Crystal Jewelry Inspiration

from the
CREATE YOUR STYLE
Ambassadors

Crystal Jewelry Inspiration

from the
CREATE YOUR STYLE
Ambassadors

CREATE
YOUR STYLE
with SWAROVSKI ELEMENTS

Ambassador

Compiled by
Karin Van Voorhees

KALMBACH BOOKS

Kalmbach Books
21027 Crossroads Circle
Waukesha, Wisconsin 53186
www.Kalmbach.com/Books

Published in 2013
17 16 15 14 13   1 2 3 4 5

Manufactured in China

ISBN: 978-0-87116-701-9
EISBN: 978-0-87116-737-8

Editor: Karin Van Voorhees
Art Director: Lisa Bergman
Layout Artist: Lisa Schroeder
Illustrator: Kellie Jaeger
Photographer: William Zuback

Library of Congress Cataloging-in-Publication Data
Crystal jewelry inspiration from the Create your style ambassadors / compiled by
  Karin Van Voorhees.

    p. : ill. (chiefly col.) ; cm.

  Issued also as an ebook.
  "Create your Style with Swarovski Elements ambassador."
  ISBN: 978-0-87116-701-9

  1. Jewelry making. 2. Crystals. 3. Beadworkers. I. Van Voorhees, Karin.

TT860 .C79 2013
745.594/2

The Swarovski Tradition

A visionary and humanist, Daniel Swarovski aimed to constantly improve on what was good, and believed that there was no future without history. More than a century later, *Swarovski*, the Austrian, family-owned and run company, produces precision-cut crystal of the highest quality, pays homage to its rich heritage, and continues to be inspired by the spirit of its founder.

Daniel Swarovski

Daniel Swarovski (1862-1956) grew up in Georgenthal, a small village in Northern Bohemia, near the center of Bohemia's flourishing crystal and costume jewelry industry. He trained as a crystal cutter and apprenticed to his father and to other local craftsmen, but before long he showed himself to be a pioneering innovator with a love of ideas, experimentation, and machines. With great foresight, he realized that embracing new technology (such as electricity) was the way to advance. He began setting crystal stones in metal for jewelry, and despite his rural location, his work connected him to the urban world of fashion, design, and jewelry. At 18, he took his first invention—a machine for setting crystal stones—to Paris, the pulse of fashion and design; cementing the link between technology and artistry that has long since characterized the company.

In 1883, at the age of 21, he visited the International Electric Exhibition in Vienna—a visit that sparked the idea that was to change his life and the history of fashion jewelry. Fascinated by electricity and by innovations presented at the Exhibition by names like Siemens and Edison, and determined to unleash the full potential of crystal, Swarovski set out to invent the first mechanical method for cutting and polishing crystal stones. He worked ceaselessly to develop his idea. After nine years, he was ready to register a patent for a machine which, for the first time, cut crystal jewelry stones to perfection.

In 1895, Swarovski moved his young family to Wattens, Tyrol, Austria, to keep his invention away from prying eyes and to harness the area's hydroelectric power for his factory. An additional advantage to the new location was a direct train link to Paris. In 1895, Daniel Swarovski, his brother-in-law, Franz Weis, and a customer from Paris, Armand Kosmann, founded the Swarovski company. The flamboyant cities of central Europe—Prague, Budapest, Bucharest, Vienna—with their mix of Eastern and Western influences, were alive with art, music, literature, science, and intellectual brilliance. Vienna, the *City of Dreams*, was a city that contrasted baroque beauty with radical art movements like the *Wiener Sezession*, aimed at making good design available to all. The extraordinary cultural melting-pot of *Mittel Europa* of this time, with its mix of historicism and modernism, is a vital part of Swarovski's heritage.

The Birth of an Industry

The first Swarovski crystal stones—the *chatons*—were more perfectly and precisely faceted and more consistently sparkling than any seen before, and gave crystal an entirely new identity for the 20th century. A huge and immediate success, Swarovski's new crystals glittered their way across the world on clothes, jewelry, hair ornaments, and shoe buckles, and the company prospered and expanded. In 1908, Swarovski, now joined in business by his three sons, Wilhelm, Friedrich, and Alfred, set up his own laboratories specifically to manufacture raw crystal material. By 1913, he had found the perfect recipe and was able to refine and improve the crystal, aiming at an unrivalled lustrous brilliance. A little later still, he experimented with color, ensuring that crystal was indissolubly linked to fashion. Dedicated to continual innovation, Daniel Swarovski's mission was to ennoble crystal and to show it as a creative material in its own right—*innovative* rather than imitative—with spectacular vitality and endless versatility.

Crystal in Fashion

As the concept of couture evolved with the new century, Daniel Swarovski and his sons began to work closely with talented couturiers including Chanel, Schiaparelli, Balenciaga, and later Christian Dior. The same creative synergy existed between Swarovski and leading couture jewelry workshops, such as Robert Goossens and Francis Winter in Paris, and embroidery ateliers, including the celebrated Maison Lesage. By the 1920s, the Jazz Age brought a lust for luxury, and Swarovski crystal was a vital ingredient feeding the frenzy—perfect for the shimmering dance dresses smothered with crystal beads that caught the light and swayed seductively. Light-filled and dramatic, the new Swarovski crystal possessed a star quality that drew the attention of celebrities and style icons. Catching the limelight, crystal made dazzling appearances in music halls and cabarets, glinting on the elaborate costumes of artists including the famous chanteuse Mistinguette, and provocative, American-in-Paris jazz singer Josephine Baker. Swarovski expanded its repertoire of crystal jewelry stones and beads, and in 1931, during the mania for crystal-encrusted couture, set up a special department for crystal trimmings, launching a readymade fabric band of crystal stones for decorating cocktail dresses, shoes, belts, bridal

"Daniel Swarovski's mission was to show (crystal) as a creative material in its own right—*innovative* rather than imitative."

gowns, and cabaret costumes. Swarovski crystal scintillated on and off stage and screen, worn by Hollywood idols like Marlene Dietrich, Marilyn Monroe, and Audrey Hepburn. Swarovski's continual exploration and innovation became a driving force within the fashion and jewelry industries.

Christian Dior and the Aurora Borealis

In the mid 1950s, Christian Dior, the protean talent of Paris couture and the creator of the revolutionary *New Look*, turned to Swarovski for a totally new expression of crystal and jewelry to complement his stunningly feminine clothes. Dior himself worked closely with Manfred Swarovski, grandson of the founder, and with Francis Winter, who ran one of the leading Parisian costume jewelry ateliers. His inspiration was the splendor of the 18th century and the grandeur and glamour of Versailles. Swarovski experimented ceaselessly, and developed a special coating that transformed a crystal stone with lightning flashes of rainbow colors. The thrilling effect recalled the Northern Lights and the stone became known as *Aurora Borealis*—a phenomenal worldwide success that continues unabated today.

A Future Built on History

From these beginnings, as the spirit and determination of the founder were handed down through the generations of his family, the company has been powered by a drive towards continual experimentation and innovation, in both design and technology. A firm belief in continual progress, and in improving and perfecting what has gone before, has been an integral part of the company's philosophy, history, and heritage.

Today, the company is still family-owned and is run by fifth-generation family members. It has a global reach with 26,100 employees and a presence in more than 120 countries. Swarovski comprises two major businesses: one producing and selling loose elements to the industry, and the other creating design-driven finished products. Swarovski crystals have become an essential ingredient of international design. Since 1965 the company has also catered to the fine-jewelry industry with precision-cut genuine gemstones and created stones. Showing the creativity that lies at the heart of the company, Swarovski's own brand lines of accessories, jewelry, and home décor items are sold through more than 2,200 retail outlets worldwide.

The CREATE YOUR STYLE with SWAROVSKI ELEMENTS Ambassador Program

Igniting inspiration…delightfully expressing style…nurturing creativity—these traits drive the CREATE YOUR STYLE with SWAROVSKI ELEMENTS Ambassadors. Bound by a common love for sparkling crystals, this elite group includes masters of a wide variety of jewelry-making techniques such as elaborate seed bead stitching, sophisticated stringing, bold metal and wirework, creative textile and fabric art, mixed media, collage, and more.

Recruited from a field of well-known craft designers, the Ambassadors foster the premium and artistic image of CREATE YOUR STYLE with SWAROVSKI ELEMENTS in their work. Their passion for designing with SWAROVSKI ELEMENTS, paired with their desire to share their knowledge and creativity with a wide audience, is reflected in the classes and workshops they teach. Personal contact with Ambassadors helps students learn the many advantages of working with SWAROVSKI ELEMENTS, proving expert instruction can lift design and craft skills to an entirely new level.

These professionals are opinion leaders and innovators in the craft and hobby industry. Many are published authors, and most teach classes and workshops on a regional or national basis. CREATE YOUR STYLE with SWAROVSKI ELEMENTS has worked closely to select the most gifted experts to join its ambassador program.

Initially introduced in February 2009 in Tucson, Ariz. (USA), the program has expanded and now includes 49 members from the United States, Germany, Japan, Canada, Mexico, South Korea, Taiwan, Belgium, France, Nigeria, Israel, Thailand, and South Africa. Wide-ranging cultural and geographic influences bring new interpretations and exciting variations of jewelry design to the work presented through this thriving program.

The CREATE YOUR STYLE with SWAROVSKI ELEMENTS Ambassador program is an extension of the CREATE YOUR STYLE website (CREATE-YOUR-STYLE.com) and sparkling community—a global online community that connects crystal connoisseurs and brings together like-minded people with a passion for self-expression through designing with crystals. In tune with the ongoing mission of SWAROVSKI ELEMENTS to nurture creativity, this community serves as an inspirational and interactive platform for the exchange of ideas, experiences, and technical and style tips. Because ambassadors are active bloggers and forum participants, enthusiasts have an open line of communication with industry experts. Additionally, jewelry makers can learn more about SWAROVSKI ELEMENTS by browsing new collections, colors, cuts, and products. The web community provides access to news and information about the brand's wide range of associated activities. It is a rich source of creative and technical support with a constant flow of news and information about fabrication techniques, design directions, design contests, seminars, and events.

The Swarovski Tradition

The CREATE YOUR STYLE with SWAROVSKI ELEMENTS Ambassador Program

AMBASSADORS & THEIR DESIGNS

Introduction

Have you ever noticed how a tiny 3mm Swarovski crystal—expertly placed in a dangling earring—can send a flash of fiery light across a crowded room? These precision-cut pretties are a designer's darling: Whether she's styling a delicate necklace with subtle accents or he's creating a fully embellished statement piece, jewelry designers understand that integrating the best elements with the best techniques gives the best results for not just the jewelry, but also for the person who will wear it for years to come.

Compiling this book and working with the Swarovski team and the CREATE YOUR STYLE with SWAROVSKI Ambassadors was an honor and a thrill. Talent runs deep among the ambassador team, and each project is brilliant in design and execution. During the editing process, I'd unwrap a piece of jewelry and have it by my computer as I carefully counted each bead and verified the directions on the screen. As I worked, I felt I got to know each and every designer through her or his piece. My appreciation for the technical accuracy, ingenious construction, and judicious use of color and elements grew as I made my way through the book. It is impossible for me to pick a favorite: Each project has revealed new insights and each ambassador has inspired me in numerous ways.

What I most enjoy about this impressive collection is the multitude of techniques and variety of styles represented—proving that crystals are not just appropriate on the dressiest occasions, but are perfect for everyday wear as well. You'll find stringing, bead stitching, wirework, metalwork, fiber arts, mixed media, resin, metal clay, and more. The projects assume a working knowledge of the technique involved. (If you are unclear about a certain procedure, technique, or stitch, consult another source to brush up on basic skills.) Detailed crystal, material, and tool lists accompany each project to help you most accurately replicate the work. Creativity is encouraged, so explore the wide range of SWAROVSKI ELEMENTS to bring your own personal flair to a project. Should you encounter difficulty finding a specific shape or color, please substitute a similar element, as there will be subtle shifts in availability from year to year.

Now it's your turn to explore. I hope you find unexpected joy as you traverse these pages. Seeking inspiration? Page through the projects and absorb the color and shine. Let your mind wander as you absorb rich textures and detailed designs. Visit the international gallery for a world tour of jewelry made by ambassadors from around the globe. Looking for personal growth? Challenge yourself with a new technique. Curious about the style makers leading design trends? Read the ambassador profiles and interviews to learn how they've built a livelihood from a passion.

This book is bursting with ideas—where will you begin?

Karin Van Voorhees

DESIGNS

Czarina

Diane Whiting

This project is a collection of some of my favorite things: Chessboard flatbacks, sew-on stones, round beads, pearls, and metal filigree. I asked myself, "What if I try to combine and layer some of the filigrees with the SWAROVSKI ELEMENTS?" and "What if I wrapped the round beads in seed beads?" The result is an opulent neckpiece that reminds me of Russian royalty, so I named it "Czarina."

materials

SWAROVSKI ELEMENTS

- **4** 18x9mm 3223 navette sew-on stone
- 14mm 2035 chessboard flatback
- **232** 3mm 5810 Crystal Pearls
- 5000 round
  - **16** 8mm
  - **2** 6mm
  - **4** 4mm

Other Supplies

- **5** round filigree components
- **4** fleur-de-lis filigree components
- **1,000** 11º seed beads
- **2** wire guards
- S-hook clasp
- beading thread (6 lb. test or size D), smoke
- beading needle
- jewelry cement or two-part epoxy

Pendant

1 Whipstitch the filigree pieces together with beading thread as shown. Stitch four round components together (**a**) and stitch four fleur-de-lis components to the fifth round component (**b**). The red lines are stitching points.

2 With jewelry cement or two-part epoxy, adhere the chessboard flatback to the center of the fifth component (**c**). Dry completely.

hint Clamp the flatback to the filigree with a clothespin while the glue is drying.

3 Place a navette sew-on stone across the join of two filigree pieces, and whipstitch (**d**). Repeat with the remaining three navette sew-on stones.

4 String approximately 55 11º seed beads. Circle around the outer edge of the navettes. Add or subtract beads to fit snugly against the crystals. Pick up the strand, sew through all the beads again, and tie a double knot. Sew through a few more beads and hide the knot. Replace the ring around the navettes. Sew down through an open space in the filigree and back up through the next closest hole (make sure the thread crosses a piece of metal in the back). Stitch through 8–10 11ºs, and repeat until the entire ring of beads is tacked down (**e**).

5 String 36 3mm Crystal Pearls. Place along the outside edge of the seed bead ring and add or subtract beads as necessary to fit snugly. Secure the ring as you did in step 4.

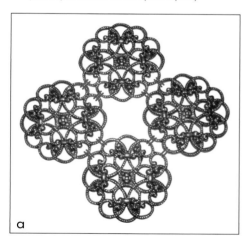
a

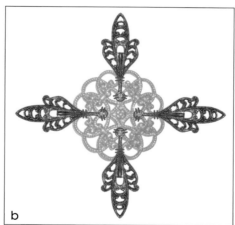
b

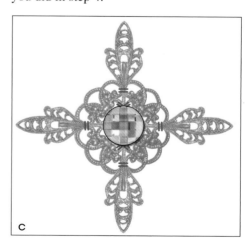
c

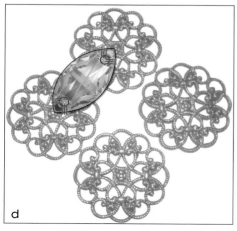
d

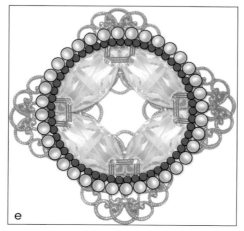
e

f

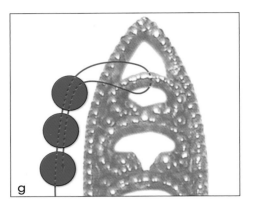

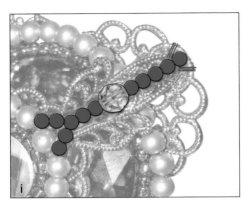

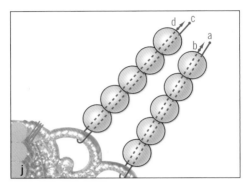

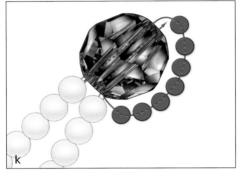

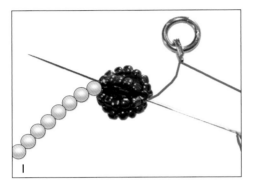

6 Pick up approximately 22 11° seed beads to make a ring, and attach around the chessboard flatback as in step 4 .

7 Using 16 3mm Crystal Pearls, make and attach a ring around the seed beads as in step 4. Position a pearl directly below the stem of each fleur-de-lis filigree. Sew through the pearls until you can exit one pearl to the right of a fleur-de-lis stem (**f**).

8 Pick up five 11°s, a 4mm round, and five 11°s. Sew down through the top hole of the fleur-de-lis filigree (**g**). Sew back up through the next hole in the filigree and go back through the five 11°s, the 4mm, and three 11°s.

9 Pick up two 11°s. Skip a pearl to the left, and sew through the next three pearls (**h**).

10 Repeat Steps 8 and 9 to embellish the remaining three "branches" of the filigree overlay. Sew through a few adjacent pearls and down through the filigree to bring the thread to the back. Tie off and cut.

11 Using roundnose pliers, gently bend the tips of the fleur-de-lis filigrees toward the back. Test-fit the overlay on the base unit.

Tips should fit into the center arcs of the base unit. Whipstitch the tips in place (**i**).

Neckband

12 On a new doubled piece of beading thread, string nine 3mm round pearls, and sew through the far right opening in the top of the finished filigree pendant (**j, a–b**). Sew back through nine pearls, and tie a square knot with the tail and working threads.

13 String eight 3mm pearls and sew through the opening in the filigree to the right of the previous opening (**c–d**). Sew back through all eight pearls, and tie a square knot as you did in step 12.

14 String an 8mm round bead and seven 11°s. Slide the beads snugly against the two pearl groups, and sew back through the crystal (**k**). Pull thread tight so the 11°s wrap around the 8mm. Repeat this stitch seven more times for a total of eight times around the 8mm.

15 String nine 3mm Crystal Pearls, an 8mm, and seven 11°s. Slide all the beads snugly against the previous caged 8mm, and sew back through the 8mm as you did in step 14. Pull the thread tight so the

11°s wrap around the 8mm. Pick up seven 11°s, and sew back through the 8mm in the same manner seven times for a total of eight times around the 8mm.

16 Repeat step 15 to create a total of eight caged 8mms with nine 3mms between each 8mm.

17 String nine pearls, a 6mm round bead, and six 11°s. Slide all the beads snugly against the previous caged 8mm, and sew back through the 6mm as you did in step 14. Pull the thread tight so the 11°s wrap around the 6mm. Pick up six 11°s, and sew back through the 6mm in the same manner for a total of six times around the 6mm.

18 To add the clasp, sew through a wire guardian and one ring of the clasp (**l**). Nest the clasp ring inside the wire guard, and sew back through the 6mm caged bead. Tie a double half-hitch knot, sew back up through the 6mm bead and the wire guard; then sew back through the 6mm and three or four pearls. Tie a double half-hitch knot, and sew through a few pearls to bury the knot. Cut the thread.

19 Repeat Steps 12–18 on the other end.

Diane Whiting discovered Swarovski Elements in 2001 and began her beading career by entering the first CREATE YOUR STYLE with SWAROVSKI ELEMENTS Design Competition. When her Crystal Iris Purse design was selected as a finalist, she was encouraged to continue, and the following year her Crystal Bow Purse won first place in the Amateur Division. She was one of the first members of the CREATE YOUR STYLE Sparkling Community, won first place in the community's design competition, and is now a moderator of the group. As a trainer in the hospitality and transportation industries, Dianne made an easy transition to teaching her innovative designs featuring SWAROVSKI ELEMENTS. Diane now teaches, lectures, and demonstrates nationally, and has been published multiple times in major beading publications.

create-your-style.com/Content.Node/ ambassadors/Diane-Whiting.en.php

"... allow yourself to not be good right away."

How long have you been making jewelry?
I began making jewelry in 2001 and knew immediately that I wanted to make a living this way. I knew for certain that I would make it my livelihood in 2009.

Best advice you've received?
It is more than just jewelry-making advice, more like life advice that I can relate to jewelry making as well, I recently received from one of my fellow Ambassadors: "The things that keep us moving forward to realize our goals are the same things that hold others back."

Favorite tool?
My needle and thread—everything happens with them!

Best thing about being an Ambassador?
Sharing my love of the finest crystal beads and elements and the company that produces them! Passing on the innovation and generosity of the company.

Favorite of the SWAROVSKI ELEMENTS?
Please don't make me chose a favorite! I love them all!

Inspiration?
The shapes and colors of all the SWAROVSKI ELEMENTS and the possibility of "what if?"

Advice for new beaders?
Two things: First, remember you are learning; allow yourself to not be good right away. Second, ask yourself "what if I ...?" and then go find the answer.

Ribbons

Tamara Honaman

The design for this metal clay ring (on paper) started in one place and, through construction, led to another. It was entertaining to be a spectator as this transpired, and I thoroughly enjoyed working out the intricacies of the design—the length of the ribbons and how best to create them, the size of the straw to lend support while the metal clay dried, the dimension of space to leave in the center to fit the Swarovski briolette, and so on. It all boils down to a formula, and once you have the formula figured out, you can make changes to accommodate the variables. The fun is in experimenting and seeing all the amazing designs that result from the experimentation.

materials

SWAROVSKI ELEMENTS
- 18mm 5040 briolette, Denim Blue

Other Supplies
- **60–75** grams metal clay
- 10 grams metal clay slip
- 5 in. 16-gauge fine-silver wire

Tools
- roundnose pliers
- flatnose pliers
- wire cutters
- olive oil
- roller
- slats or playing cards
- flexible nonstick sheet
- 20–25mm circle cutter
- spray bottle filled with water
- scissors
- tissue blade
- ring sizer
- ring mandrel and holder
- clear adhesive tape
- drinking straw
- extruder
- rubber-tipped tool
- paintbrush
- mug warmer
- sanding sponges and polishing papers
- hammer
- steel bench block
- kiln with kiln shelf
- vermiculite
- brass brush
- tumbler with mixed stainless steel shot
- burnishing compound (or water and dish detergent)

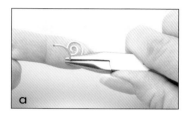
a

b

c

d

e

f

1 Using roundnose pliers, make a plain loop on the end of the 16-gauge wire. Using flatnose pliers, spiral the wire for three turns. With flatnose pliers, make a 90-degree bend in the wire tail (**a**).

2 Apply a light coating of olive oil to your tools, work surface, roller, circle cutter and the edge of the tissue blade. Roll out 10 grams of metal clay to 3 cards (.75mm) thick. Use a circle cutter to cut out a 20–25mm circle. Wrap the excess clay to keep it moist.

3 Place the spiral in the metal clay slip and coat the wire with a thick layer. Place the spiral on the center of the clay circle (**b**).

4 Roll 5–8 grams of clay to 2 cards (.5mm) thick. Cut out a 20–25mm circle, and then cut the circle in half. Wrap the excess clay to keep it moist; if needed, apply a mist of water. Using a paintbrush, apply water to the circle, working around the spiral and the metal clay slip. Place each half circle on top of the spiral so they meet in the middle. Apply pressure to join the halves as well as seam the two circles together, capturing the wire spiral (**c**).

5 Use the ring sizer to determine the size of your ring. Increase by 2½ sizes to allow for the

shrinkage that occurs when firing metal clay. Cut a strip of flexible nonstick sheet. Place the sheet on the ring mandrel at the increased size. Trim the sheet so there is little overlap. Wrap the sheet around the mandrel and place a small piece of tape onto the seam of the nonstick sheet. Burnish the tape to create a bond and so the seam is nearly invisible. Any bump in the nonstick sheet will transfer to the ring band.

6 Roll 20g of clay to 6 cards (1.5mm) thick and in a long, thin rectangle. Trim the long edges of the rectangle to create the width of the band. Keep the edges as straight as possible.

7 Wrap the clay around the mandrel at the designated size so the ends overlap. Hold the blade on an angle and cut through both layers of clay (**d**). Remove the excess clay from each end.

8 Using a paintbrush, apply slip to both angled ends. Join the ends and apply a bit of pressure to secure. Using a damp paintbrush, clean up any excess slip. Dry the band to semi-dry.

9 Carefully remove the nonstick sheet and ring from the mandrel. Place the nonstick sheet, with the ring still in place, on a mug warmer and dry completely. Carefully press inward on the seam of the nonstick

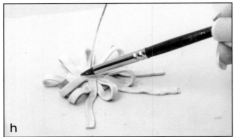

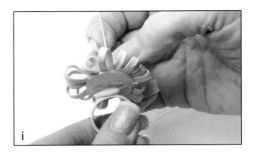

sheet to remove the sheet from the band. Dry the clay further, if needed.

10 Cut the drinking straw into 12.5–19mm (½–¾ in.) pieces. Place 15 grams of clay into the extruder. Fit the end of the extruder with a rectangle disk. Extrude a ribbon of clay onto a nonstick sheet (**e**). Unfurl the ribbon, if needed.

11 Using a paintbrush, wet half the circle from the wire toward the edge. Place the end of the extruded ribbon on the clay circle. Cut the ribbon to about 51mm (2 in.) long. Repeat adding four ribbons on half the circle so they radiate out from the center like spokes.

12 Place a straw piece in the center of one ribbon. Fold the end over the straw and place on the clay circle near the start of the next ribbon (**f**).

note Leave the ribbon flat or give it a slight twist.

Repeat for the next two ribbons. Mist the fourth ribbon with water. Repeat adding ribbons to the other half of the circle. Fold the ribbon ends until you reach the beginning (**g**).

13 Carefully transfer the nonstick sheet onto the mug warmer and dry until at least semi-dry. Add a second layer of ribbons (**h**). Dry the ring base completely.

14 Using a paintbrush, apply slip to any gaps. Dry completely.

15 Using sanding sponges and polishing papers, and working in progressive grits, carefully refine the ribbons. Refine all areas: top, bottom, and inside the curls. Apply slip to any gaps and dry completely. Sand and refine as needed.

16 Using sanding sponges and polishing papers, and working in progressive grits, carefully refine the surface of the ring band. Refine all areas inside and out. Apply slip to any gaps and dry completely. Sand and refine as needed.

17 Place the ring flat onto a sanding sponge. Carefully move the ring band in a figure-eight motion on the sanding sponge to create a flat edge. Repeat on the other edge.

18 Using polishing papers, round the edge along the inside and outside of the ring band so the ring fits comfortably.

19 Wet the ring band seam, extending about 10mm (⅜ in.) in each direction. Place 3–5g of clay on the wet area, shaping the clay to fit the width of the band. Apply a layer of slip to the center of the ribbon base. Place the ribbon base onto the wet clay so the base is centered (**i**). Sure up the wet clay so it meets the ribbon base cleanly. If needed, add more clay.

Apply more water and clean up the join. Dry completely.

20 Add more clay if needed. Dry completely. Using sanding sponges and polishing papers, refine the clay to create a nearly perfect finish. Place the ring in a bed of vermiculite inside the kiln. Fire the kiln at FULL speed to 1650°F (899°C) and hold at this temperature for two hours. This will ensure the strongest possible finish. Cool to room temperature.

21 Using a brass brush and soapy water, brush the surface of the ring, getting into all areas. Place in a tumbler with mixed stainless steel shot and burnishing compound. Tumble for 30 minutes to overnight until the finish is as you desire. Clean the ring with soap and water.

22 String the briolette bead on the wire. Trim the wire so it extends 25.5mm (1 in.) above the rondelle (**j**). Carefully hammer the end of the wire to flatten about 6–8mm (¼–⁵⁄₁₆ in.). Using roundnose pliers, turn a small loop on the end (**k**). Using flatnose pliers, continue to spiral the wire until it meets the surface of the crystal. Leave the spiral standing straight up (**l**), or carefully press it flat onto the surface of the crystal.

Tamara Honaman is a jewelry designer who also loves to teach and share her designs through various media. She works SWAROVSKI ELEMENTS into her metal clay, wire, and beaded designs. Tamara is the founding editor of *Step-by-Step Beads*; former editor of *Step-by-Step Wire* and "Step-by-Step" in *Lapidary Journal;* and one of the founders of the national show *Bead Fest*. Currently she contributes projects, articles, and designs to Fire Mountain Gems and Beads, producer of her full-length DVD, *Secrets to Art Clay Success*. Tamara has appeared on several seasons of the series *Beads, Baubles & Jewels* and on the DIY program *Jewelry Making*. She contributes projects to magazines and books.

create-your-style.com/Content.Node/ ambassadors/Tamara-Honaman.en.php

"Know no bounds and believe you can."

How long have you been making jewelry?
Almost 20 years. I used to make items for gifts. When I got an order for nine bracelets, I knew I was on to something and never looked back.

Best advice you've received?
Know no bounds and believe you can. Don't be afraid to try something new.

Favorite tool?
I'm a tool junkie, so this is a tough one—tools with power are high on the list! I love the Jooltool because it makes polishing easy. I love my flex shaft as it makes drilling and polishing easy and convenient.

Best thing about being an Ambassador?
Working with crystals is the obvious answer, so I'll go to the next level—I love working with the diverse group of artists, the camaraderie we have, the sharing nature of everyone, and all the wonderful people we get to work with at Swarovski. And of course, I love sharing designs and ideas with everyone who also loves Swarovski and the chance I have to educate those who are less familiar with all the wonderful products.

Favorite of the SWAROVSKI ELEMENTS?
I'm in love with the 5041 large-hole faceted briolette; I have always been drawn to the shape. The facets on this beads are mesmerizing; the colors, mouthwatering.

Inspiration?
Color, the ocean, my children's laughter, the sheer delight of trying something new and failing so I can keep trying.

Advice for new beaders?
Follow your heart, follow your passions, believe you can, and never be afraid to ask for help.

Check It Out

Lisa Pavelka

Creating a dramatic checked pattern

of crystal within crystal is much easier than you may think. This elegant and graphic project is just one of many variations that you can create when combining air-hardening epoxy clay and crystals. Swarovski Cosmic Ring components offer nearly limitless creative potential when combined with moldable materials. Since the introduction of the Cosmic components line, the availability of new colors, shapes, and sizes has expanded wonderfully. The open centers are the perfect canvas for showcasing a mix of materials and, of course, even more crystals. Regardless of your experience, it's easy to achieve professional-quality results and nearly instant gratification following these simple steps.

materials

SWAROVSKI ELEMENTS
- 30mm 4439 square ring, Crystal CAL V SI
- **24** 2mm 4428 Xilion square stones, Crystal
- **25** 1100 PP6 Xilion chatons, Light Siam

Other Supplies
- Crystal Clay two-part epoxy clay, black
- Find-Its glue-type bail

Tools
- ½ tsp. craft-dedicated measuring spoon
- disposable gloves
- needle tool or toothpick
- fine-tip tweezers
- polymer clay blade
- ball-tip stylus
- rubbing alcohol and cotton cloth
- optional: piece of silicone cookie-sheet liner

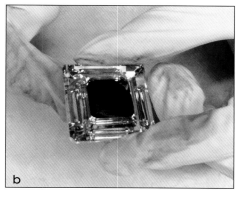

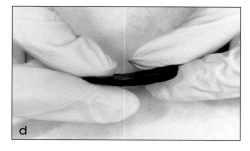

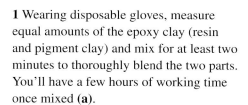

1 Wearing disposable gloves, measure equal amounts of the epoxy clay (resin and pigment clay) and mix for at least two minutes to thoroughly blend the two parts. You'll have a few hours of working time once mixed (**a**).

2 Roll half of the mixed clay into a ball and press into the center of the crystal. You may have to add or remove clay. The center should be filled so that it levels off when smoothed with your finger and lies flat, just below the first angled interior bezel edge (**b**).

3 Cover the epoxy clay with a checkerboard pattern of 49 crystals in all (seven rows of seven crystals each): Lightly poke seven holes along one edge, evenly spaced. Use the tweezers to place and press alternating square (Crystal) and round (Light Siam) stones along this first row. Continue to add six more rows, alternating the color of the first stones in

each new line to form the checkerboard pattern (**c**).

4 Roll the remaining epoxy clay into a ball. With your gloved hands, flatten the ball and shape it into a square that's approximately the same size as the crystal ring (**d**).

tip if you're not in a hurry to create your pendant, you might want to start by mixing half the recommended amount of clay and preparing only the inlaid insert first, allowing the clay to harden for 3–4 hours. Then complete steps 5 and 6 after mixing fresh epoxy clay for the back. Allowing the center clay to harden first will make adding the back easier and reduce the risk or marring the front checkerboard design.

5 Press the flattened clay onto the back of the crystal and trim the excess with the blade (**e**).

6 Press the bail into the clay in the corner for an angled suspension as shown, (**f**), or in the middle of one side for a square orientation when worn. Roll the excess clay into a ball and press it over the base of the bail to secure it. Texture the back by stippling he ball-tip stylus over the surface of the clay. Trim the edges along the back with the clay blade after texturing. The excess clay can be used to reinforce the area around the bail base. Air cure the piece overnight before wearing.

7 Clean any clay residue from the crystal surface with a soft cloth dipped into rubbing alcohol. You can do this before or after the clay has hardened.

design variations

With so many shapes and sizes of Cosmic Rings, you'll want to create several variations. Here are some tips for those shown:

Floating Orb

Roll a small ball of black epoxy clay and press it into the center of a 33x24mm Cosmic Oval (4137, Crystal), leaving a third of the center open. Press a 14mm graphic fancy stone (4795, Denim Blue) into the epoxy clay so it rests against the bottom of the opening. If you'd like, roll a tiny snake of the epoxy clay and lay it along the bottom edge of the graphic fancy stone. Place and press 3–4 small Xilion chaton stones (pp6 or pp7) in clear or another color along the edge as shown. Add a simple, large jump ring or bail, and dry overnight. For a fancier look, create a bail by stringing 14 3mm 5328 bicone beads (in the color of your choice) around the open section of the cosmic oval to hang the pendant from.

Blue Lagoon

Create this piece in a similar fashion to the Check It Out pendant. I used a 30mm Crystal (4437, Crystal CAL V SI) and a mix various sizes of chaton stones in a range of blues mixed with clear. The closer the stones are, the more overall impact the finished piece will have.

Lisa Pavelka is an award-winning artist, author, and designer who has worked professionally for over two decades with mixed mediums including polymer and metal clays, resin, wire, and crystal to name a few. She teaches at workshops, on creative cruises, and leads professional seminars for artists internationally. Lisa is a regular contributor to and columnist for numerous magazines and makes frequent TV appearances on shows such as HGTV's *Carol Duvall Show*, DIY Network's *Jewelry Making*, Discovery Channel, JTV, and more. In addition, she has authored four books and two DVDs. Her line of creative products is distributed internationally.

lisapavelka.com
create-your-style.com/Content.Node/
ambassadors/Lisa-Pavelka.en.php

"My hands are the most versatile and essential tool I have."

How long have you been making jewelry?
I've been making jewelry and other types of artwork since 1986. I didn't realize that it would become my career until around 1998. Prior to that, my priority was to be at home with my children and then go back to a career producing and directing television. Creating jewelry and artwork was a way to work part-time from home and supplement our income doing something I was passionate about.

Best advice you've received?
To always leave an open jump ring in any necklace or bracelet I make, so that there is a point where the piece could easily break if it got caught on something. This is such an important safety consideration, and I am surprised at how many professionals I encounter don't know this tip.

Favorite tool?
My hands are the most versatile and essential tools I have. I rely on so many other tools and devices, but anything that can't be done with your hands eliminates some of the tactile intuition that working with your hands alone can offer. Otherwise, I choose my cordless Dremel Stylus drill. I hardly go a day without using it.

Best thing about being an Ambassador?
The opportunity to spread the joy of creating with crystal to a wider audience, thanks to the support the program offers, and the network of friends and I've made among my colleagues. It's an amazingly talented and diverse group of designers!

Favorite of the SWAROVSKI ELEMENTS?
Any of the Cosmic Rings, especially the 20mm or larger components. They are incredibly versatile for many creative applications including focal pieces, decorative frames, and toggles.

Inspiration?
Just about everything I see! I find inspiration everywhere; in nature, textile patterns and texture, etc. I keep a binder of clippings, sketches, and concepts that I go to when looking for instant creative inspiration. I find with so much that intrigues me, I seldom need to refer to the book, but it's nice to know it's there.

Advice for new beaders?
Don't worry about finding your style. Concentrate on becoming proficient at the mediums and techniques you are drawn to first. With mastery, you'll find your voice emerges naturally! Also, don't be afraid to share and lend inspiration to others. Having an open and giving approach to sharing your work will provide an abundance of rewards in your creative journey.

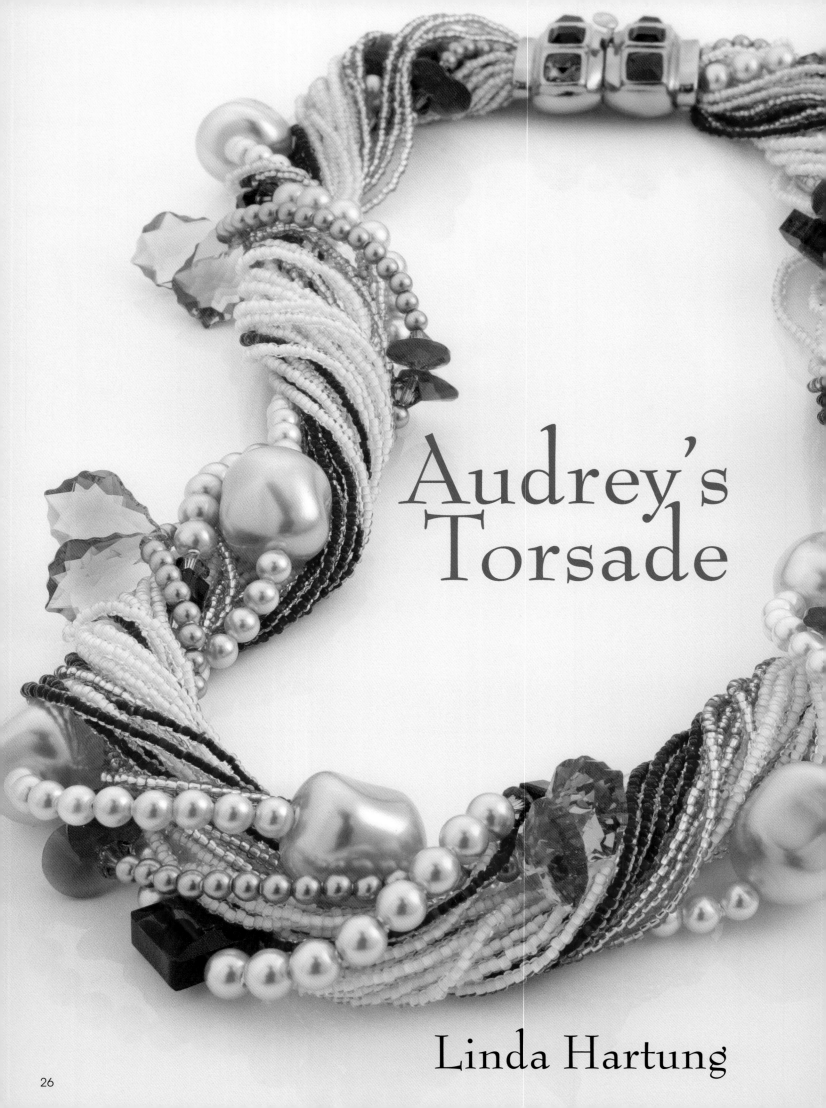

Audrey's Torsade

Linda Hartung

A torsade necklace style is worn by twisting it multiple times and then clasping it. The style is luxurious, elegant, and stylish, and offers the opportunity to easily change crystal shapes and mix colors. One simply has to put on a torsade necklace to understand its allure and popularity. My mother especially loves torsades, and since she is one of my biggest customers, I named this one after her.

materials

SWAROVSKI ELEMENTS

- **9** 14mm 5840 baroque pearls, Crystal Light Gold Pearl
- **5** 10mm 5624 stairway beads, Amethyst
- **10** 16x11mm 6090 baroque pendants, Light Amethyst
- **10** 8mm 6428 Xilion pendants, Cyclamen Opal
- **20** 4mm 5328 Xilion beads, Tanzanite
- **5** 4mm 5601 cube beads, Purple Velvet
- 5810 pearls
  79 5mm Gold
  94 4mm Cream
  149 3mm Bright Gold
- 4428 Xillion squares
  2 5mm Amethyst
  2 5mm Cyclamen Opal
  2 5mm Tanzanite

Other Supplies

- **27** grams 14º Italian glass seed beads, butter cream (15 strands/20 in.)
- **9** grams 14º Italian glass seed beads, purple (5 strands/20 in.)
- **9** grams 14º Italian glass seed beads, gold (5 strands/20 in.)

- multistrand windows Alacarte clasp, gold plate (gold)
- 6½ ft. 19-strand .018 flexible beading wire, gold plate
- 40 ft. 1X Hastings bonded nylon bead cord, white
- **2** 2 in. medium-weight headpins, gold plate
- **8** 2x2mm crimp tubes, gold plate
- **2** 3.5mm crimp tubes, gold plate

Tools

- chainnose pliers
- flush-cut wire cutters
- jeweler's tweezers
- toothpick for mixing epoxy
- bamboo skewer and Tac-it putty (optional for picking up crystals)
- G-S Hypo Cement
- two-part all-purpose clear-drying epoxy

please note, this necklace is based on a 20½-in. length including the clasp. Twisting can shorten the length about ½ in.

Seed Bead Strands

You will string 25 20-in. strands of 14º seed beads on a permanent, non-stretch bead cord (**a**). Allow 6 in. of extra cord on each end.

1 For the base color (butter cream), make 15 strands (three groups of five strands). Gather one group (five strands) and make an overhand knot with all the cords at one end to secure.

2 Slide the beads down to the knot. Check that all strands are the same length. Make a loose overhand knot at the end. With tweezers, grab all the strands inside the loose square knot next to the beads (**b, inset**). Tighten the knot to the base of beads (**b**).

3 Repeat steps 1 and 2 to make five strands (one group of five) of the accent color (purple). Repeat steps 1 and 2 to make five strands (one group of five) of the metal highlight color (gold).

Accent Strands

You will make three 20-in. accent strands (**c**). The key is to follow a pattern so that when all the strands are twisted

together, the large focal pieces do not overlap or come too close to the clasp end and are evenly distributed.

4 On flexible beading wire, place a 2x2mm crimp 3 in. from the wire end and flatten.

5 String 11 4mm Cream pearls, *a 14mm Light Gold baroque pearl, and nine 4mm Cream pearls*. Repeat from * to * eight times, making sure the baroque pearls begin at the 2-in. mark and are placed every 2 in.: 2-4-6-8-10-12-14-16-18.

6 String 11 4mm Cream pearls.

7 String a 2x2mm crimp. For flexibility and to avoid overtightening, hold the strand vertically and let gravity remove the slack. Make a flattened crimp next to the last pearl and do not apply downward pressure. Leave a 3-in wire tail.

8 Cut a 26-in. piece of beading wire. Place a 2x2mm crimp 3 in. from the end and flatten.

9 String seven 3mm Bright Gold pearls.

a

b

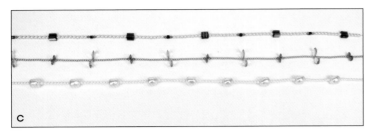

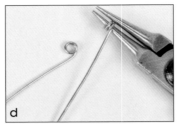

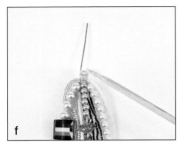

10 String two 16x11mm Light Amethyst baroque pendants, 15 3mm Bright Gold pearls, a 4mm Tanzanite Xilion bead, two 8mm Cyclamen Opal Xilion pendants, a 4mm Tanzanite, and 15 3mm pearls. Repeat until the beaded portion is almost 20 in. long. Make sure the baroque pendants start at the 1-in. mark and repeat every 4 in.: 1-5-9-13-17.

11 String six 4mm pearls and check the length, adjusting with 4mm pearls if necessary to reach 20 in.

12 String a 2x2mm crimp. Hold the strand vertically and let gravity remove the slack. Make a flattened crimp next to the last pearl and do not apply downward pressure. Leave a 3-in. wire tail.

13 Cut a 26-in. piece of wire. Place a 2x2mm crimp 3 in. from the wire end and flatten.

14 String three 5mm Gold pearls, a 4mm Tanzanite Xilion bead, a 4mm Purple Velvet cube, a 4mm Tanzanite Xilion, and eight 5mm Gold pearls.

15 String a 10mm Amethyst stairway bead, eight 5mm Gold pearls, a 4mm Tanzanite Xilion bead, a 4mm Purple Velvet cube, a 4mm Tanzanite Xilion, and eight 5mm Gold pearls. Repeat this pattern until the beaded portion is almost 20 in. long, making sure that the 10mm stairway bead starts at the 3-in. mark and repeats every 4 in.: 3-7-11-15-19.

16 String four 5mm gold pearls.

17 String a 2x2mm crimp. Hold the strand vertically and let gravity remove the slack. Make a flattened crimp next to the last pearl and do not apply downward pressure. Leave a 3-in. wire tail.

tip Be sure to gather the same sides together, when finishing, otherwise your pattern will be different.

Finish the necklace

18 Trim the head from a headpin. Make a double loop at the end smaller than a 3.5mm crimp (**d**). Make two.

19 Gather all the seed bead groups together. Twist the ends together and secure with G-S Hypo Cement to create a needle. Over all the strands, slide a double-looped headpin and a 3.5mm crimp snug to the base of the seed beads.

20 Insert each accent strand through the 3.5mm crimp, and then string a 2x2mm crimp over all three accent strands (**e**). Remove the slack and flatten the 2x2mm crimp.

21 Pull each seed bead cord end to remove all slack. Flatten the 3.5mm crimp with chainnose pliers. Turn over and squeeze the 3.5mm crimp again from the other side.

22 At the base of the 3.5mm crimp, bend the headpin to a 90-degree angle. Mix two-part epoxy and apply it to the cord ends and the 2x2 crimp holding the accent strands (**f**). Trim the cord and wire ends.

23 Mix two-part epoxy and apply a thin bead of glue around the inside rim of the clasp. Position a Xilion square crystal in the rim. Follow the color pattern shown (**g**). Dry.

24 Insert the headpin into a clasp end/hole (**h**). Pull the headpin to fill the clasp end. Make sure the strands are tucked inside the clasp. With pliers, twist the headpin at the base of the clasp, tightening all the strands into the clasp and forming a small loop to keep the headpin from pulling through (**i**).

25 Trim the headpin and test to make sure the clasp closes properly. Apply two-part epoxy over the headpin loop for added security.

26 Repeat steps 24 and 25 on the other side.

tip To work around the internal box in the other side of the clasp, you may need to squeeze the double loop with chainnose pliers to make it more oval shaped.

Linda Hartung is co-owner of and designer for Alacarte Clasps, WireLace, and WireLuxe. Her jewelry lines, Linda Arline Originals and Alacarte Jewellery, carry the branding *Made with SWAROVSKI ELEMENTS*. Linda is passionate about teaching, designing, and creating innovative techniques that she loves sharing with others. Her designs have been featured on the cover of MJSA Journal, *Bead Style*, and *Bead Unique* publications. She has published numerous other projects in bead and art jewelry magazines around the world.

alacartejewelry.com
alacarteclasps.com
wirelace.com
wireluxe.com
create-your-style.com/Content.Node/
ambassadors/Linda-Hartung.en.php

"Sometimes you just have to let yourself play and see what comes."

How long have you been making jewelry?
If you count looking for rocks with holes in them and using my shoestrings to turn them into a necklace—then that would be some 50-plus years! It became my livelihood when it became our sole source of income.

Best advice you've received?
Accept criticism and compliments—it's a chance to view things from someone else's eyes.

Favorite tool?
My brain, because it works 24 hours a day, seven days a week. Some of my best designs come in my sleep.

Best thing about being an Ambassador?
Having direct access to the full range of SWAROVSKI ELEMENTS as well as the ongoing education I receive is invaluable. I can then pass along this education through teaching and design projects to motivate and inspire others.

Favorite of the SWAROVSKI ELEMENTS?
Are you kidding? It changes with every new release. They're all fabulous.

Inspiration?
Jesus.

Advice for new beaders?
To understand that not every design starts with a vision. Sometimes you just have to let yourself play and see what comes. I often doodle with whatever is sitting on my desk and that sparks a new color combination, technique, or small part of what can be incorporated into a larger piece.

Stepping Stones

Diane Fitzgerald

The Stepping Stones Bracelet is made with African Circle Stitch, a very old and typical Zulu technique that I recreated by studying a piece found in the Russell-Coates Museum in Bournemouth, England (shown below). Many of the Zulu stitches that I've documented look fantastic when worked with SWAROVSKI ELEMENTS.

materials

(for a 7½-in./19cm) bracelet)
SWAROVSKI ELEMENTS

- **5328** bicones
    - **272** 3mm color A, Tanzanite AB
      (alternate: Pacific Opal AB)
    - **188** 4mm color B, Padparadscha
      AB 2x (alternate: Metallic Blue 2x)
    - **80** 4mm color C, Violet Opal
      (alternate: Aurum)

Other Supplies

- **3** grams 15º seed beads
- 30mm 5-strand clasp (loops 5mm apart)
- Fireline, 6 lb. test, crystal
- **2** #12 beading needles
- match or lighter

1 Thread a needle on 3 yds. of thread. Bring the ends together and wax well. Knot, trim tails 1mm from the knot and melt the knot slightly with a flame.

2 Pick up four color A 3mm bicones. Pass the beads to within 1 in. of the knot. Separate the strands between the beads and the knot and pass the needle between the strands. Sew back through all four beads **(figure 1)**.

3 Pick up a 15º seed bead. Pass under the first loop on the clasp, back through the 15º, and through the next bicone to the right **(figure 2)**.

4 Pick up a 15º, a color B 4mm bicone, and a 15º. Pass under the next loop on the clasp and back through the 15º.

5 Add three Bs and sew up through the B added in the previous step, then continue through the first B added in this step (forming a circle) **(figure 3)**.

6 Continue across the row, repeating steps 3 and 4 with the following pattern: four As, four Bs, and four As. Each time on step 3 you will add the first bead of the next set of four bicones.

7 At the end of the row, pass through one more bicone so your thread exits at the bottom. Turn the work so the working thread is exiting on the left. Continue with row 2 of the pattern in step 9 for the next row.

8 With thread exiting between the two bottom bicones, pick up a 15º and four Bs. Sew back through the 15º. Pass the thread from back to front under the thread

figure 1

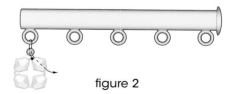

figure 2

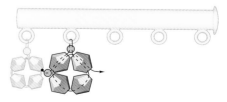

figure 3

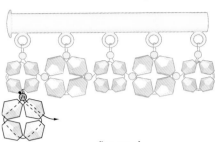

figure 4

figure 6

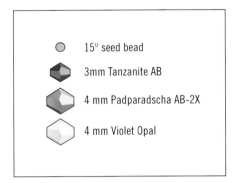

- ⬡ 15° seed bead
- ⬣ 3mm Tanzanite AB
- ⬢ 4 mm Padparadscha AB-2X
- ⬡ 4 mm Violet Opal

between the two bicones above (like doing brick stitch); then sew back through the 15° and the bicone to the right (**figure 4**).

9 Repeat step 8 for the desired length following the color pattern in **figure 5**. The color pattern for the four repeat rows is:
Row 1: A - B - A - B - A
Row 2: C - A - B - A - C
Row 3: A - B - A - B - A
Row 4: B - A - C - A - B

10 Sew the other side of the clasp to the end of the bracelet as shown in **figure 6**.

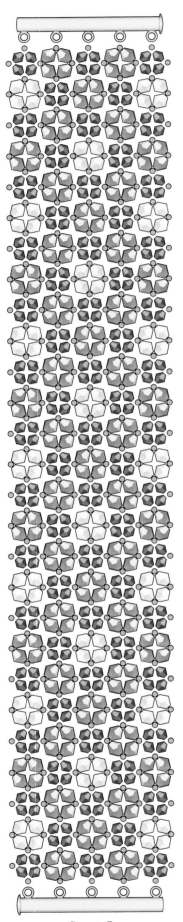

figure 5

Diane Fitzgerald Degrees in journalism and design and a career in public relations provided a platform from which Diane launched her bead design enterprise, Beautiful Beads. This endeavor included a short stint in retail, designing jewelry for classes, and writing 12 books and over 100 magazine articles. After more than 20 years designing and teaching, she still finds these little bits of glass as enticing as the day she strung her first beads. Their color, shapes, luminescence, and versatility beckon and make her fingers itch to weave them into new and wondrous jewelry. Diane's travel has been transformed into searching out the nooks and crannies of London's Portobello Road, the bead factories of Czech Republic and Japan, and the beaders of South Africa to learn the never-ending story of beads.

create-your-style.com/Content.Node/ambassadors/Diane-Fitzgerald.en.php

"If I like the look, I go for it."

How long have you been making jewelry?
I've been beading since 1988. I began to depend on it for my income in 1995 when I turned my back on my career in public relations.

Best advice you've received?
Don't follow the trends, create them.

Favorite tool?
My favorite tool is my needle. Without a needle, it would be nearly impossible to do beadwork.

Best thing about being an Ambassador?
The best part of being an ambassador for me is exploring a new area of beads, their history, their variety, how the colors interact, and how the shapes can be used to create new forms and combine with other forms.

Favorite of the SWAROVSKI ELEMENTS?
Without a doubt, and perhaps not too surprisingly, it is the bicone because of its versatility.

Inspiration?
Inspiration can pop up anywhere and I am constantly on the lookout for it. Inspiration for me does not come from a single category of things but more from the world and all that is in it in general. This includes the natural world and the constructed world—both contemporary and historical. I see something and it triggers my mind to translate it into beads. If I like the look, I go for it.

Advice for new beaders?
Learn about color and design. Courses on these topics have been the most help to me of everything I've learned.

Cornucopia

Sandra Lupo

Inspiration was timely—I recently visited the site of the Temple of Artemis in ancient Greece (now Turkey), and I was impressed with the architectural structure of the temple, consisting of 127 fluted stone columns. This necklace design is built on the concept of a repeated element—the Artemis bead paired with coiled wire cones—integrating beautifully in a bounty of geometric shape, size, and color. Precious gold-filled wires embrace the beads, and balled sterling silver wires add a fanciful dimension. Prong-set fancy stones, sparkling cosmic squares, cosmic circles, and luscious crystal pearls complete this design.

materials

SWAROVSKI ELEMENTS

- 20mm 4437 cosmic square fancy stone, Crystal CAL V SI
- 20mm 4139 cosmic ring fancy stone, Crystal Sahara
- **4** 3mm 5328 Xilion, Olivine
- 5540 Artemis
    - **3** 17mm Dark Indigo
    - **2** 17mm Crystal Copper
    - **2** 17mm Olivine
    - **2** 12mm Dark Indigo
    - **7** 12mm Crystal Copper
    - **5** 12mm Olivine
    - **6** 12mm Crystal
- 4161 long classical oval fancy stones:
    - 15x5mm Olivine
    - 15x5mm Jonquil
    - 15x5mm Crystal
- 5810 Crystal Pearl
    - **14** 10mm Crystal Night Blue
    - **14** 6mm Crystal Night Blue

Other Supplies

- **3** 15x5mm 4161/S H2 O prong setting
- 77 ft. 26-gauge gold-filled wire, dead soft
- 10 ft. 20-gauge sterling silver wire, half-hard
- 2½ ft. 20-gauge sterling silver wire, dead soft
- 1½ ft. 18-gauge sterling silver wire, dead soft

- 21mm toggle clasp (bar only), sterling silver
- 2-in. 24-gauge 1.5mm ball-tip headpin, sterling silver
- .018-.019 diameter flexible beading wire, 49 strands, silver plated
- **2** crimp beads, sterling silver
- **2** crimp covers, sterling silver
- **2** wire guards
- **3** 4mm ID 18-gauge jump rings, sterling silver
- 7.5mm ID 18-gauge, jump ring, sterling silver
- **9** bead bumpers, plastic

Tools

- roundnose pliers
- chainnose pliers
- flatnose pliers
- bentnose pliers
- crimping pliers
- stone setting pliers (optional)
- nylon jaw pliers
- flush cutters
- needle files
- polishing cloth
- manual coiling tool or cordless automatic drill
- 8-9mm diameter cone mandrels
- safety glasses
- butane or propane torch

Preparation

Make in advance:

1 Balled wire: Cut six 6-in. pieces of 20-gauge and two 7-in. pieces of 18-gauge sterling silver wire. Use a torch to ball one end of each piece. Clean and polish. Set aside.

2 Wrapped Loop Pearl: String a 10mm pearl onto a 2-in. ball-tip headpin and make a wrapped loop. Extend the wraps to the top of the pearl for a swirled cap. Set aside.

3 Open and Close Jump Rings: Open three 4mm ID jump rings. Set aside. Open the 7.5mm jump ring, pick up the cosmic square ring, and close the jump ring. Set aside.

4 Set the Fancy Stones: Use prong setting pliers, or chain-nose pliers with care, to avoid scratches or breaks. Insert the stone squarely into the setting. Tighten one of the four prongs with the setting pliers, and then tighten the opposite diagonal prong. Repeat with the remaining prongs. Repeat to make three fancy stones. Set aside (**a**).

5 Form the Coiled Wire: Use a manual winder or a cordless automatic drill to wind 26-gauge gold-filled (GF) dead-soft coils on a 20-gauge sterling silver (SS) half-hard core wire (**b**). From these coiled lengths, cones will be made in different sizes (**c**). Exact measurements are given in steps 6–10.

tip Wear safety glasses and use caution when using machinery, wire, and mandrels. Maintain a slow speed for even control.

6 Cut an 8-in. piece of 20-gauge SS wire for the core. Secure in the chuck. Working from the spool, wrap the end of the 26-gauge GF wire on the core wire. Wind the GF wire on the core wire to make a 5-in. coil. Cut the GF wire from the coil. Remove the core wire from the chuck.

7 Repeat step 6 five times to make a total of six 5-in. coils to be used with the 17mm Artemis beads. Set aside.

8 Repeat step 6 using a 6-in. piece of 20-gauge SS wire for the core and winding 26-gauge GF wire to make a 3-in. coil. Make a total of six 3-in. coils to be used with the 12mm Artemis beads. Set aside.

9 Repeat step 6 using a 5-in. piece of 20-gauge wire for the core wire and winding 26-gauge GF wire to make a 2-in. coil. Make a total of four 2-in. coils.

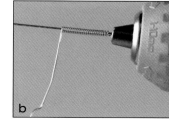

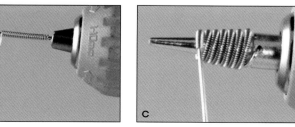

a b c

d

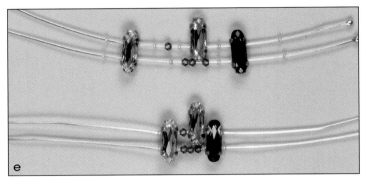

e

f

g

wire—it will form 1–2 rounds. Continue to wind as the GF coil forms on the mandrel (**c**).

13 Use chainnose or flatnose pliers to hold the SS core wire end to help form the coil into a cone. Remove from the chuck. Set aside.

Each coil will be used between two 10mm pearls as shown in (**d**). Set aside.

10 Repeat step 6 using a 12-in. piece of 20-gauge SS wire for the core wire and winding 26-gauge GF wire to make an 8-in. coil. This piece will be used with the 17mm Dark Indigo Artemis bead used at the bottom of the dangle.

11 Form the Coiled Cones: Insert an 8–9mm diameter cone-shaped mandrel into the chuck of the manual winder or cordless automatic drill.

12 Add the exposed core wire of one length of coiled wire made in Form the Coiled Wire. Slowly wind the SS core

14 Repeat steps 11–13 for each coiled wire length. Pair the coils with the crystals and set aside (**d**).

Assemble the Base Necklace

15 String the beads and coiled cones on a 30-in. piece of flexible beading wire (see photo, p. 34, for bead order).

16 On each end, string a crimp bead and a wire guard. Go back through the crimp beads. Crimp the crimp beads and cover with bead covers.

17 On one end, attach a 4mm ID jump ring to the wire guard. Open a 4mm ID jump ring, string the closed ring and the toggle bar. Close the jump ring.

18 On the other end, on a 4.5mm ID jump ring, string the wire guard and the 7.5mm jump ring on the Cosmic Square Ring. Close securely. Set the necklace aside.

Create the Dangle

19 String a bead bumper on a balled wire from step 1. Repeat with a second wire.

tip The plastic bead bumpers align the metal and crystal components carefully, leaving no space between metal parts.

20 String the Olivine fancy stone over both wires. String a bead bumper on each wire.

21 String three 3mm Xilion beads and a bead bumper on one wire.

22 String the Jonquil fancy stone, a bead bumper, a 3mm Xilion bead, and a bead bumper on the other wire.

23 String the Crystal fancy stone over both wires. String a bead bumper on each wire.

24 Gently push the components together on both wires so they are about 1½ in. from each ball tip. Set aside (**e**).

Wirewrap the Upper Dangle Segment

25 Wrap the balled wire component with the set fancy stones into the square cosmic ring with the 1½ in. of wire between the stones and the ball tips. Position the two 1½-in. sections through the square cosmic ring and with your fingers, loosely wrap each wire two or three times. Face the ball tips out from the square ring.

26 Gently push the compressed fancy set stone section up towards the square ring. The plastic bead bumpers will set the compression.

27 With ½ in. on each wire at the base of the compressed fancy set stone section, wrap the component into the round cosmic ring. Create two full wraps with each wire (**f**).

28 Trim excess wire at the back of the round ring and press gently against the ring.

29 Cut a 3-in. piece of ball-tipped wire and with your fingers, wrap the cut end horizontally between the bottom of the fancy stone section and the top of the round ring. As you complete the wrapping, bring the ball tip out from the round ring.

30 Compress the horizontal wraps with a nylon jaw pliers for a flattened effect (**f**).

Wirewrap the Lower Dangle Segment

31 String the 7-in. ball-tip wire through the round ring, leaving a 1½ in. tail. Wrap the tail end one or two times around the round ring, and end with the ball tip facing out (**g**).

32 String a 12mm Artemis and its coiled cone, another 12mm Artemis and its coiled cone, and a 17mm Artemis and its coiled cone. Push the coiled beads toward the round ring.

33 Trim the 18-gauge SS wire and make a plain loop. Open the loop, string the Crystal pearl dangle, and close the loop.

Sandra Lupo teaches wire techniques for jewelry making at the Newark Museum Arts Workshop, N. J., and at local, national and international events. As an Ambassador for Create Your Style with Swarovski Elements she has been an instructor for the CYS show in Tucson since 2006. She has done technical editing for Kalmbach Publishing Co. and others. Sandra's designs have been published in *Beading with Crystals, Beading with Pearls,* and *Wire Style* and her design, "Valley of the Queen," was featured on the cover of Fire Mountain Gems and Beads Jewelry Maker's Catalog of Best Sellers for 2010/2011. She is on Fire Mountain's Ask the Experts Team and her video tutorials can be viewed at the Fire Mountain website.

Sandsstones.com
Sandra@sandsstones.com
create-your-style.com/Content.Node/
ambassadors/Sandra-Lupo.en.php

"Appreciate your talent; appreciate your life."

How long have you been making jewelry?
I suppose I have been a jewelry maker since I was a young girl, playing with my grandmother's jewelry box baubles and beads. My grandfather was a fine jewelry artist and the love for jewelry was inherent in our family. My own path in the DIY market came about 20 years ago when I soldered my first brass finger ring and set it with a stone. I did not expect to make this a livelihood. I was conscientious in following my passion, my love for jewelry making, designing, instructing and sharing.

Best advice you've received?
In design, to be aware of my surroundings and build on my experiences. In execution, to use basic, solid techniques and push the limits.

Favorite tool?
Half-round forming pliers. This tool allows me to work wire without marring the creation I've made. Although a slender tool, it is strong enough for me to move metal. Second to that is a bent-nose pliers because it is truly an extension of your fingers. It tucks wire ends nicely.

Best thing about being an Ambassador?
Certainly working with the Create Your Style Team, both nationally and internationally. I am proud to be a CYS Ambassador representing the best quality crystal product. The sparkle of Swarovski Elements wowed me with my first crystal creation, many years ago. I also enjoy the camaraderie of my fellow Ambassadors and look forward to any opportunity to work with the entire team.

Favorite of the SWAROVSKI ELEMENTS?
In creating this necklace, I have been smitten with the Artemis Bead. Up to now, my love affair has been with the faceted teardrop briolette and faceted teardrop pendant. However, I am awed by all of the Innovations Pendants. My favorite color is Erinite, but new colors like Antique Rose and effects such as Golden Shadow and Silver Shade will always find their place in my designs.

Inspiration?
I am inspired by the beauty of nature, the great outdoors, and my travels and experiences. My students and my jewelry making peers inspire me also. There is a great give and take in this community.

Advice for new beaders?
Follow a path that you set out for yourself. Learn all you can and share what you discover. Appreciate your talent; appreciate your life. Embrace your creativity. Laugh a lot!

Little Black Dress Approved

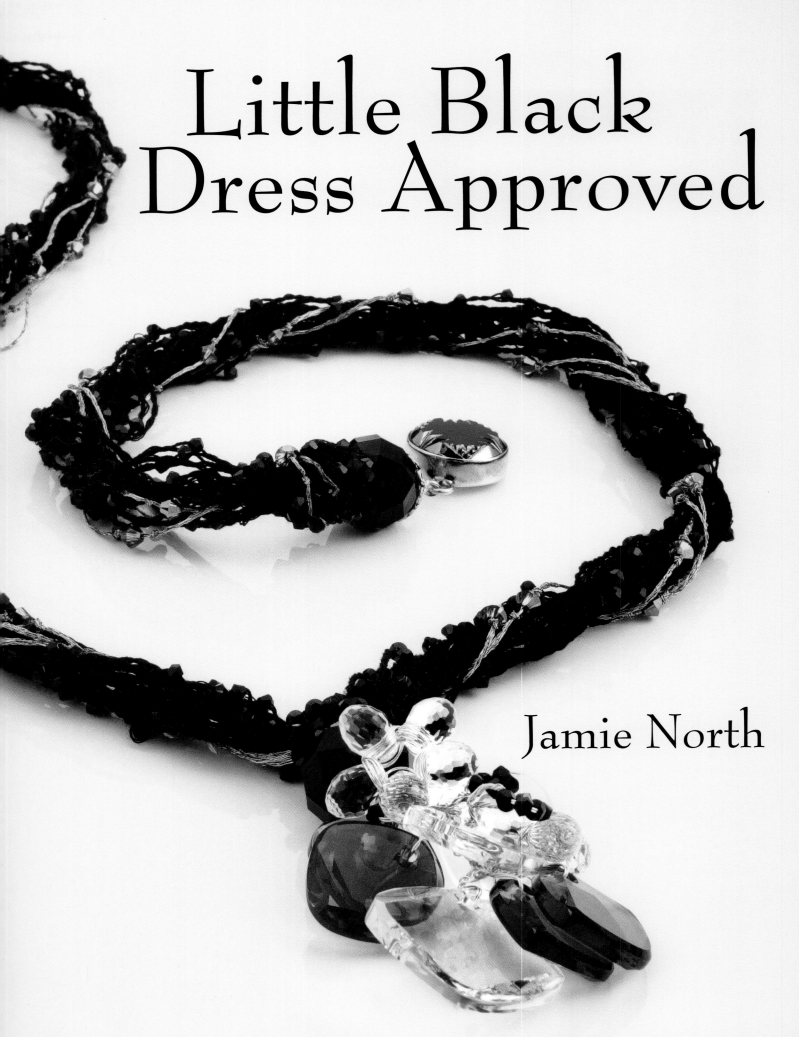

Jamie North

Long, lean and perfect for your little black dress, this dazzling and elegant necklace is opera length and will add a touch of class to any evening out. The clean, sophisticated lines of Swarovski's metro pendants are stunning. The free-form pendant makes for one-of-a-kind styling; you'll end up with a custom creation. So fun to make and never duplicated!

materials

SWAROVSKI ELEMENTS

- **60–72** 4mm 5328 Xilion bicones, Crystal Silver Night
- **6** 10X7mm 6002 pendant, Crystal
- **3** 18mm 5041 large hole rondelles, Jet
- 6058 Metro Pendant
    - 25mm Crystal
    - **2** 18mm Crystal
    - **4** 18mm Black Diamond
- Crystal yarn, Jet

Other Supplies

- **2** bead caps
- box clasp
- 1mm WireLace, titanium
- 28-gauge wire
- G-S Hypo cement
- toothpick

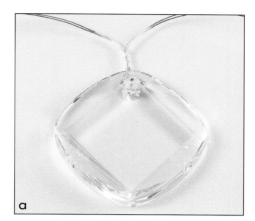
a

b

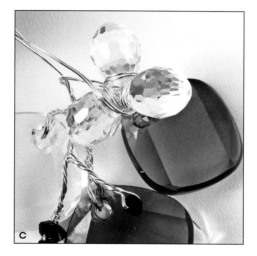
c

d

Create the Necklace

1 String 20–26 4mm Xilion bicones onto the WireLace.

2 Tie an overhand knot in the WireLace approximately 3 in. from the end. Slide a 4mm bead toward the knot and tie another overhand knot as close as possible to the bead to hold it in place.

3 Leave a 1–2-in. space (no need to measure), tie an overhand knot in the WireLace, slide a 4mm to the knot, and tie a knot to hold the bead in place.

4 Continue until the WireLace strand is approximately 6 in. longer than the desired length of your finished piece.

5 Repeat steps 1–4 to make two additional strands (my necklace is 33 in. long, so my strands were about 39 in. long).

6 Cut 9–12 separate lengths of crystal yarn approximately 6 in. longer than the desired length of your finished piece (I used 39-in. pieces).

7 Gather one end of all strands together and tie an overhand knot about 3 in. from the end.

8 Loosely twist the strands together. Tie an overhand knot on the other end.

9 Cut four pieces of 28-gauge wire, each 10–12-in. long.

10 String two pieces of 28-gauge wire through the knot and pull the ends together to capture the knot.

11 Pull off any of the beads on the strand ends—these will be used when creating the pendant portion of your necklace.

12 Pull each strand tightly to snug up the knot.

13 Pass the wire and ends of the yarn through one of the large-hole rondelles.

14 Apply a small amount of G-S Hypo cement into the knot to secure. Trim the yarn ends.

15 String the wires through the bead cap. Treat the wires as one and make wrapped loop to connect to an end of the box clasp.

16 Repeat on the other end.

Create the Pendant
17 Cut approximately 6 ft. of 28-gauge wire and fold in half.

18 Center the large metro pendant on the doubled wire, pinch over the top of the pendant, and twist all wires together a few times to secure (**a**).

19 Pass one end of the doubled wire through a smaller metro pendant and twist. (This will allow the smaller pendant to layer on top of the larger metro pendant but not scratch or rub on it) (**b**).

20 Twist all strands of wire together for approximately ¼–½ in. Add another small metro pendant, dangling crystal pendant, or other flower (**c**).

21 To create a large flower with the drops, string the wire through five crystal pendants (article 6002) twice, and then wrap the outside over and under to secure.

22 To create a small flower with the 4mm bicones (previously removed from the yarn), string the wire through five of the beads and twist.

23 Add various branches, flowers and crystals by twisting the wires together until you have created a free-form pendant (**d**).

24 Use a toothpick to curl any branches, dangles, and/or stems.

Create the Bail and Assembly
25 Cut a 3-ft. piece of 28-gauge wire and fold in half.

26 Pass the wire under the top of the pendant and center the pendant on the fold.

27 Cut a piece of leftover black yarn and center the pendant on the yarn (**e**).

28 String both wire and black yarn ends through a large-holed rondelle.

29 Wrap the wire around the center of the necklace a few times to secure (**f**). Cover the wraps with the black yarn. Tie the ends and tuck them in.

30 Create several twisted "stems" with the rest of the wire to embellish the bail (**g**).

Optional
31 To keep the yarn from twisting, place it on a towel, apply steam with a regular iron, and allow to cool completely.

Jamie North is very proud to have been part of the CREATE YOUR STYLE with Swarovski Elements Ambassador program since its inception. Jamie's flair for "random order" and creating beautiful pieces using simple techniques is her trademark and her designs are often described as elegant, fun, versatile, eclectic, and always very wearable. She is an accomplished instructor and has had projects published in many beading magazines. Jamie has one grown son and lives in Calgary, Alberta, Canada, with her life-partner, Kevin, and their fur babies.

GlitznKitz.com
create-your-style.com/Content.Node/
ambassadors/JAMIE.NORTH.en.php.

"Being surrounded by the incredible talent and creativity of the other ambassadors is amazing."

How long have you been making jewelry?
My first published piece was in 2008 but I had been making jewelry for about four years before that. Livelihood? It's my passion, but I'll let you know when it becomes my livelihood.

Best advice you've received?
Proper finishing lifts your pieces from homemade to professional. Don't underestimate the impact of the smaller details.

Favorite tool?
It's a toss up between nylon-jawed pliers and my Tronex wire nippers. I have about eight pairs of nylon-jawed pliers so there are always some within reach. My nippers are fine tipped and sharp so I can get really close for a nice finish.

Best thing about being an Ambassador?
I love it all! Being surrounded by the incredible talent and creativity of the other ambassadors is just amazing. There is great energy within the group! I also really like hearing and seeing the new shapes and colors and the trend highlights. It gets the imagination humming with ideas!

Favorite of the SWAROVSKI ELEMENTS?
There are so very many of them that I absolutely LOVE, but I have to say that I always come back to the Xilion bead. It is such a versatile shape and comes in so many sizes and colors. I also adore anything from the Cosmic and Graphic series … and the Wild Hearts are simply stunning!

Inspiration?
I struggle to define a specific thing that inspires me. Inspiration is everywhere! I love texture, free-flowing shapes, colors I see in nature, architecture, and fabrics.

Advice for new beaders?
Never stop learning new things—even if you do become specialized in a particular area. No one is that much of an expert! Even if something isn't your style—you can learn from it and appreciate the technique and creativity involved, which in turn makes you a better artist and designer.

Tribal
Princess

Pat Riesenburger

Fiber jewelry has become increasing popular as more jewelry designers and textile artists discover this versatile and tactile medium. There is something particularly appealing about the play of sparkling Swarovski crystal against the warmth of handmade felt. The best part is that high style does not have to mean exorbitant cost. A few grams of fiber and some sparkling crystal elements are all you need to create a couture jewelry creation!

materials

SWAROVSKI ELEMENTS
- **5–6** 27mm, 16mm, or 18mm 1122 rivoli
- Assortment of 3mm 3128 crystal sequins including Smoked Topaz, Olivine, Jet, Crystal Copper
- An assortment of ss30 flatback loose rhinestones including Gunmetal and Topaz
- An assortment of ss34 rose montees, Topaz.
- An assortment of tiny embellishment crystals such as 2mm 5000 rounds, 3mm 5810 pearls, 2.5mm 5328 bicones
- 20 yds. (approx.) 59000 crystal cotton yarn
- **2** 3015 crystal buttons

Additional Supplies
- **3–4** grams seed beads
- 15 grams wool roving
- Silk embroidery floss
- Silk ribbon
- Ultrasuede for bracelet back
- Fireline beading thread
- Hand towel
- Container of hot water
- Tulle or other netting
- Olive oil soap solution
- Bubble wrap or felting mat
- #12 beading needle
- Embroidery needle
- 2–2.5mm crochet hook

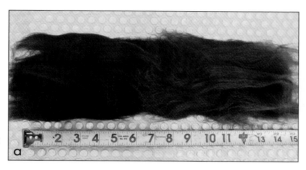

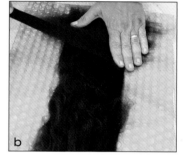

1 Place a towel and bubble wrap (bubble-side up) on a work surface. Pull a tuft of fiber and place it on the bubble wrap. Add tufts from left to right, overlapping the edges (called shingling). The fiber will shrink about 25–30% during felting, so work larger to plan for shrinkage (**a**).

2 Make a second layer of shingles perpendicular to the first. Hold the fiber in your left hand with your right hand about 8 in. away (**b**). Pull the roving apart (without exerting pressure).Place a third layer of shingles perpendicular to the second.

3 Add rivolis: Make a cushion—or nest—from a bit of fiber for each rivoli (**c**).The extra fiber prevents sharp edges from popping through the back.

4 Completely cover the stones with more fiber to capture them and keep them in place (**d**). You'll be doing a lot of rubbing to turn the fiber into felted fabric, so cover the rivolis well.

tip Put a bit of colored fiber on the back (**e**) so you know the orientation when you cut open the stones (photo page 44).

5 Cover with netting. Sprinkle liberally with warm water and soap solution.

6 Gently rub your hands on top of the fibers to distribute the soapy water (**f**), keeping the stones in place as you rub. There is no need to "roll" the fiber as is typically done with wet felting. Your hands will get the job done. Rub for a few minutes.

7 It's time for the pinch test. Remove the netting and pinch to see if the fiber has developed a "skin." If it comes together as one piece (**g**), the skin is forming. The crystals are still loose, so now it's time to get serious about trapping the crystals.

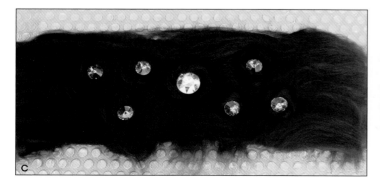

8 Rub vigorously against the bubble wrap without the netting. Keep the crystals in position **(h)** with your hands and fingers. The more you rub, the tighter the fibers become, ultimately locking the crystals in place. As the crystals become more firmly imprisoned, pick up the piece and toss it forcefully on the bubble wrap 10 times. This is called fulling and causes the fibers to both tighten and to become softer and thicker.

9 After about 10 minutes of aggressive rubbing, the crystals should be tightly embedded, but there will still be a small amount of wriggle room. Put the piece into a container of nearly boiling water.

10 When the water is cool, remove the piece. The fibers will have absorbed water and expanded (the crystals might seem looser). Don't worry. Simply give it another few minutes of vigorous rubbing and tossing and it will tighten right up! The piece has shrunk quite a bit since you started. Work until you can no longer wriggle the stones.

11 Make a small cut into the right side of the fiber in the middle crystal **(i)**. Do not make a big cut! The fiber "wound" will

expand and with a large incision, the stone may fall out. That would be a bummer after all this work! (If a crystal does fall out, use craft glue to pop it into place.)

12 With your finger, gently rub soap solution around the wound in the fiber to heal it and open up the hole. One little cut is enough to reveal your stone—just keep rubbing! Trim any stray fiber hairs with scissors. Repeat with the other crystals

13 Now for embellishment—where something pretty cool turns into something totally sublime! The process is organic and without clear rules. Every piece of felt evolves differently. I begin by working a blanket stitch around the raw edges of each embedded stone using silk floss. Circle a few stones with simple stitches for a lovely quilted effect to define them.

14 Thread a #12 beading needle with Fireline beading thread (it can withstand the sharp edges of crystal beads). The felt is thick, making it easy to hide the thread within the fiber. Although the back of the piece will not be visible and no one will see your stray threads, you might as well do it right. Try to be neat and tidy. You will feel better.

15 Now add accents! The stitching should be giving your cuff a bit of personality by now. Find negative space that is calling out for sparkle. Knot the tail, and sew up from the back. Sandwich the tail in the fluffy space between the layers, never to be seen again. Easy, peasy. Sew on 7–10 montees. Whew! You are doing it!

16 The rest of the piece will build from the placement of the first beads. For balance, I often skip around and work on opposite corners in an effort to keep color and texture complementary. One of my favorite tricks is to create a bubbly looking confection using 3mm pearls and 2mm crystal rounds grouped tightly together. I also use French knots with abandon. French knots create quite an impact when clustered together, but try using them sparingly as an accent. Use a variety of materials: silk or cotton floss, ribbon, yarn, etc. Fill in with seed beads and swirls of 3128 crystal sequins. My approach to bead embroidery is "more is better" and I wind up with a decadent piece, totally encrusted with sparkle. Sew a button or two on the edge of one side of the cuff. Leave about ¼ in. unembellished at the outer edges.

17 The pièce de résistance—Crystal Yarn. Blanket stitch around the perimeter of the cuff for a base. Crochet from the back through the blanket-stitched seam, pushing the beads to the front. In the spirit of excess, I used 20 yards of several different Swarovski yarns in single, double, and triple crochet for this piece. You are almost done! Make a crochet chain stitch button closure where appropriate and pat yourself on the back!

Pat Riesenburger is a recovering attorney who now uses her time hosting workshops in her Florida studio and playing with fiber and sparkly things. She finds something particularly appealing about the play of elegant Swarovski crystals against the warmth of handmade felt; accordingly, Pat uses SWAROVSKI ELEMENTS in most of her fiber creations whether jewelry or home décor items. She describes her style as "Folk Art meets High Society." Pat teaches workshops throughout the United States and writes a popular marketing blog, The Crafty Retailer. She sells hand dyed fibers, kits, and Swarovski Elements on her website.

UrbanStitchStudio.com
Pat@UrbanStitchStudio.com.
create-your-style.com/Content.Node/
ambassadors/Pat-Riesenburger.php

"Use colors that are outside of your normal palette; take a class; have an adventure!"

How long have you been making jewelry?
I started collecting vintage costume jewelry as a young girl and always had an appreciation for sparkle and personal adornment. However, it was not until I opened a bead store in 2000 that I actually picked up a crystal bead for the first time. Most of the work I did initially was geared toward selling classes and selling beads—very basic stuff. I sold the shop in 2005 and discovered fibers, at which point the fun really began for me. I knew immediately that my life had changed—the juxtaposition of cool sparkle and warm textile speaks to me.

Best advice you've received?
"Go where inspiration takes you." Simple words that have freed me to try new things and live outside of the box!

Favorite tool?
My hands, of course! Ragged and worn, they serve me well.

Best thing about being an Ambassador?
Access! It is all about access—to beautiful crystals, to talented jewelry designers, to a world of people passionate about the things that I enjoy.

Favorite of the SWAROVSKI ELEMENTS?
The crystal yarn, hands down! It is truly a decadent treat. Expensive, but so worth it! Almost every piece of jewelry I design includes a splash of crystal yarn…there is nothing like it when it comes to adding texture and sophistication to a cuff bracelet or necklace.

Inspiration?
There is not a specific "thing" that inspires me. Generally I find that while I am in the studio I go to a happy Zen place that affords me peace and joy. The more I work, the more wonderful ideas are birthed—it is a lovely cycle. I get the same feeling while working in the garden.

Advice for new beaders?
Play! Try something new! Use colors that are outside of your normal palette; take a class; have an adventure! Carry a portable project with you everywhere. The greater opportunity you give yourself to create, the happier you will be!

Royal Jewelry
Suite

Leslee Frumin

The two-holed bead inspired the Royal Jewelry Suite. This square bead has the holes running diagonally rather than on the square, which makes it much more interesting to design with. Coupling it with SWAROVSKI pearls and Xilion beads added the elegance I strive for. The Japanese seed beads give just enough metal to complete the design. The off-loom bead weaving technique incorporates right-angle weave with a twist. I like to design jewelry that is wearable and beautiful.

materials • earrings
SWAROVSKI ELEMENTS
- **2** 14x14mm 5180 square two-hole beads
- **12** 5mm 5810 crystal pearls
- 5328 Xilion beads
  - **2** 4mm
  - **4** 3mm

Other Supplies
- 2 earring wires
- 15º and 11º Japanese seed beads
- 6 lb. crystal Fireline
- #12 beading needle

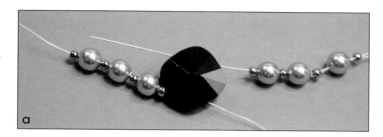

1 Thread a needle with a 40-in. piece of Fireline leaving an 8-in. tail. Pick up *an 11º seed bead and a 5mm pearl. *Repeat two times. Pick up an 11º. Pick up a two-hole bead. Pick up *11º and 5mm pearl. *Repeat two times. Pick up an 11º. Sew into the second hole of the two-hole bead as shown (**a**). Note the holes are on the diagonal.

2 Sew into the tail end and back through the entire unit formed. This helps secure the beads and prevents them from slipping. Exit an 11º with the needle pointing away from the square bead (**b**).

3 Pick up a 15º, an 11º, a 15º, a 3mm Xilion, a 15º, an 11º, and a 15º. Sew into the 11º straight across the two-hole bead (**c**). Sew through the two-hole bead and exit the next 11º in preparation for step 4.

4 Repeat step 3 on the opposite side. Sew through the two-hole bead and exit the 11º with the needle pointing away from the square bead on that side (**d**).

5 Step up through the 15º, 11º, 15º, and 3mm Xilion bead (**e**).

6 Pick up a 15º, an 11º, and a 15º. Sew into the 11º in front of the center top pearl, sew through the pearl, and exit the 11º on the other side. Pick up a 15º, an 11º, and a 15º and sew into the 3mm Xilion (in the center). Sew through the 15º, 11º, and 15º going toward the two-hole bead (**f**). Sew through the 11º and the two-hole bead, and exit the 11º on the other side. Repeat on the other side.

7 Weave through the beads and exit the center "top" pearl. Pick up four 15ºs, an 11º, a 4mm Xilion, an 11º, three 15ºs, an earring wire, and three 15ºs (**g**). Sew into the 11º closest to the working end of the thread.

Sew through the Xilion and the next 11º. Pick up four 15ºs. Sew into the opposite side of the pearl. Reweave this connection three times. End all threads with half hitch knots, and trim. Make a second earring.

tip Sewing back through creates a snug fit and keeps thread hidden. The two-hole beads have distinct sides—place beads and embellishment on the front.

The necklace is similar to the earring with right-angle weave units between. I recommend creating the base and then embellishing once the base is complete.

necklace • materials

- (16½ in. necklace)
SWAROVSKI ELEMENTS
- **20** 14x14mm 5180 square two-hole beads
- **164** 5mm 5810 pearls
- **41** 3mm 5328 Xilion beads

Other Supplies

- Japanese seed beads size 15º and 11º
- Box clasp with double connection
- French bullion wire
- 6 lb. crystal Fireline
- Size 12 beading needle

To increase the necklace length, calculate 1 in. per double-hole bead and add eight pearls for each additional double-hole bead and two Xilion beads.

tip Reweaving all of the necklace sections as they are built stabilizes the necklace and supports its weight.

1 Thread a 5-yd. piece of Fireline with a needle and leave a 2½-yd. tail. Pick up *an 11º seed bead and a pearl*. Repeat from * to * three more times. Sew into the tail end and reweave. Exit a pearl.

2 Pick up an 11º and a two-hole bead. Pick up an *11º and pearl*. Repeat two more times. Pick up an 11º. Sew into the second hole of the two-hole bead (forming the bottom of the unit) **(a)**. Snug all beads.

3 Pick up an 11º, a pearl, an 11º, a pearl, and an 11º. Sew into the pearl above the two-hole bead (forming the top of the unit).

4 Continue to sew through the 11º and the two hole bead **(b)** and reweave this RAW unit 1½ times so you exit the end 5mm pearl.

5 Exit the pearl above the second hole of the two-hole bead (where you will continue the necklace). Pick up an 11º, a pearl, an 11º, a pearl, an 11º, a pearl, and an 11º*. Sew into the opposite side of the pearl you exited **(c)**. You are creating a right-angle weave unit between the two-hole bead units .

6 Repeat steps 2–5 for the desired length of the necklace. When the thread is about 8 in., thread the needle on the tail, weave through beads to exit the end 5mm pearl, and continue the weave. Should you run out of thread, add thread with half hitch knots, burying them in the pearls.

7 Add a new thread if necessary to embellish the necklace. Exit an 11º at the top of the necklace. Pick up a 15º seed bead, an 11º, a 15º, a

3mm Xilion, a 15º, an 11º, and a 15º and sew through the next 11º at the top of the right-angle weave unit. Sew down through the pearl and exit the 11º at the bottom corner **(d)**.

8 To make the "X" design, pick up a 15º, an 11º, and a 15º. Sew into the Xilion bead **(e)**. Pick up a 15º, 11º and a 15º. Sew into the 11º at the bottom of the right angle unit **(f)**. Snug together.

9 Sew through the bottom pearl and into the 11º up through the pearl. Exit the 11º above the two-hole bead. Work as in steps 7 and 8 for the two-hole bead using the 11º seed beads that are positioned similar to the right angle units.

10 French bullion wire is a nice finish for the claps. Cut four pieces a "titch" bigger than a ¼ in. Use a 24-in. piece of Fireline doubled for strength. Sew into the end pearl of the necklace. Pick up an 11º and a piece of French wire. Pass through the clasp.

Be sure to have the right side up! Hold onto the tail.

12 Sew back into the 11º just added and sew through the end pearl.

13 Repeat steps 11–12 for the second connection. Then sew through the 11º, create a half hitch knot in front of the pearl and tug to pull the knot into the pearl. Repeat making half hitch knots in front of pearls at least 3 times. Sew the two loose ends on one needle and create knots as described.

14 Repeat steps 11–13 for the opposite end of the necklace. Be sure the clasp does not twist. I recommend that you keep the clasp closed until you have the connection complete.

Leslee Frumin, a bead and metal artist from San Juan Capistrano, Calif., teaches off-loom beadweaving and metal jewelry techniques. Leslee has published and won awards in both areas. She loves to teach, and her goal is to create a fun and successful learning experience. Her passion for all the colors and textures made possible by beads, metals, and stones keeps her excited. If Leslee could add another 24 hours to a day, to work on designs, she would be thrilled. Drawn to sparkly things, Leslee includes crystals in many of her designs.

create-your-style.com/Content.Node/
ambassadors/Leslee-Frumin.en.php

"It took me a number of years before I started creating designs of my own."

How long have you been making jewelry?
I made jewelry as a child at summer camp. I started learning metalsmithing in 1986 and added beading to my repertoire in 1994. It took me a number of years of classes before I started creating designs of my own. I honed basic skills in metals and beading before designing and teaching.

Best advice you've received?
To have patience and perseverance to create the best jewelry possible.

Favorite tool?
Those that get the job done! These can change depending on what the task is. A new one at the moment is the Tulip beading awl. It has such a fine point—it helps get out stubborn knots and mistakes!

Best thing about being an Ambassador?
The supportive relationships between all of us in the group. I also appreciate learning about the latest Swarovski Elements.

Favorite of the SWAROVSKI ELEMENTS?
I love all that glitters—beads, fancy stones, pendants etc. I especially like to combine these with the Swarovski pearls. Putting these together in elegant designs is my passion.

Inspiration?
I am inspired by many things—artists of the past like René Lalique, nature, and the materials themselves.

Advice for new beaders?
My advice to new beaders is to learn skills and techniques so you can work many designs. Stick with it—even if it seems daunting. When learning, work steps to allow yourself to learn. We all started at the beginning and had frustrating moments. That is part of learning!

Spangle

Bangle

Brenda Schweder

This Spangle Bangle design gave me a run for my designer's money! I set out to use Crystal Chaton Banding (by the way, Fern Green is my favorite green of all time!) several times with not-so-fabulous results. Nothing I attempted highlighted the crystal's color, nor featured its brilliance the way it deserved. Then, I realized that I was trying too hard. By letting the steel wire do its structural thing (and not over-working it), I achieved this minimal, but fun approach. And as a bonus, the blingy crystal rows are contrasted by the steel's deep luster; framing them and giving the co-stars equal stage time!

materials

SWAROVSKI ELEMENTS
- 9–10 in. 52500 chaton banding, Fern Green

Other Supplies
- 20–24 in. 14-gauge dark annealed steel wire
- 8 ft. 4-ply Irish waxed linen, dark brown (or slate grey)
- G-S Hypo cement

Tools
- white chalk pencil or dressmaker's chalk
- ruler
- heavy duty cutters
- chainnose or flatnose pliers
- roundnose pliers
- bench block or small anvil
- ball peen or utility hammer
- wire brush or steel wool (fine, 00)
- Renaissance wax or microcrystaline wax
- cleaning cloth
- round bracelet mandrel
- needle file

*Use tools dedicated for use with steel wire

Prepare the Wire Armatures

1 Cut two 10-in. pieces of 14-gauge steel wire. (Note: this makes a standard 8-in. inner diameter bangle. Adjust accordingly for a larger or smaller bangle.)

2 Make a plain loop at one end of one wire using the largest part of roundnose pliers.

3 Lay the wire flat on the bench block and hammer, forging about ¼-in. of the unworked end. File the tip if necessary.

4 With the largest part of roundnose pliers, on the remaining end, make a soft right-angle bend perpendicular to the loop orientation at the 1¼-in. mark.

5 Form the wire into a rough circle, bending the right angle toward the outside. Fit the loop over the right angle (**a**).

6 Finish the right angle bend to form a hook encasing the loop (**b**). (Temporarily move the loop away from the bend for a nice curved shape.)

7 Bend the tip of the hook up 45 degrees with chainnose or flatnose pliers (**c**).

8 Fit the circle over a round bracelet mandrel and hammer to form a perfect circle (**d**). Tweak the hook and loop closure with pliers to flow with the circle. Hammer flat on a bench block for additional texture and shaping.

9 Repeat steps 2–8 to form a second bangle.

10 Clean both bangles and finish with wax.

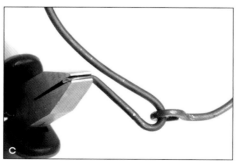

a

b

c

d

Connect the Crystal Mesh to the Armatures

11 Cut two 4-ft. pieces of waxed linen.

12 With one piece of linen, tie the first half of a square knot around one bangle and the first hole in the corner of the mesh, leaving a 6-in. tail (**e**).

13 Sew into the second hole in the same row and loop around the bangle. Thread the linen up through the loop and carefully take up the slack, tightening the stitch to the bangle edge (**f**). (The seam can be anywhere except under the hook and/or loop.)

14 Repeat step 13 with each hole in the mesh and work completely around the bangle. (You may need to trim the mesh at the end, but it's easier to work with a slightly longer piece, just in case.)

15 Fill the last hole of the row and carefully tighten the linen.

16 Repeat steps 12–15 to connect the second bangle, making sure to match the orientation of the hooks.

Zip Up and Finish the Bangle

17 Sew up through the back of the same hole as in step 15 and exit the front.

18 Create the first ladder stitch by sewing down through the same hole on the opposite (right) side and up the hole just below it (**g**). Repeat twice, if necessary, back and forth, ending up in the corner hole on the right side.

19 Continue around the bangle, through the same hole from the back again and through the loop. Pull taut.

20 Tie the working tail to the original tail (from the lower right corner) with a square knot. Keep it taut and tight to the bangle.

21 With the longer tail, create a faux knot to the left (centered below the seam in the crystal mesh) around the bangle.

22 Tie a tight square knot with this tail and the tail to the left.

23 Pick up the longer tail, and poke it through the first hole above the bottom row of crystals, just above the bottom linen ladder rung.

24 Backstitch back up around the rung and continue to the next rung up, continuing to poke, and then backstitch twice more.

25 Continue up a third time, but instead of backstitching around a linen ladder rung, loop around the top bangle, and through that loop. Pull taut.

26 Tie an overhand knot with this tail and the original from the left, keeping the knot taut and tight to the bangle.

27 Poke the tip through the last stitch around the bangle to the right and tie an overhand knot to itself taut and tight to the bangle (**h**).

28 Dot all knots with glue and dry overnight. Trim close.

Brenda Schweder is the author of *Steel Wire Jewelry, Junk to Jewelry,* and *Vintage Redux.* Her designs and fashion jewelry forecasts have been published more than 100 times in books and magazines. Schweder also pens "Creative Minds," *Wirework* magazine's column encouraging creative freedom. She teaches internationally. Catch her on Etsy, Facebook, and Twitter.

BrendaSchweder.com
create-your-style.com/Content.Node/
ambassadors/Brenda-Schweder.en.php

"Allow yourself to be happy with the process, not just the results."

How long have you been making jewelry?
I've been making jewelry since 2004, just after I began co-authoring *Bead Style* magazine's original Fashion Forecast column. I was so inspired by the idea of creating fashionable jewelry that I had to try my hand at it. I haven't looked back since. This is the only job I've had that continually challenges and fulfills my need to create!

Best advice you've received?
The best advice surrounding creating altogether is the best jewelry-making advice I ever received. Blast through to the finish. There is always a point in creation of a thing that can halt you dead in your maker's tracks. Plow through it to the other side to reach the victor's spoils!

Favorite tool?
It's the tool I've just developed: the Now That's a Jig! It's going to rock the wire jewelry world! Finally, a jig that works for, not against, the avid wire artist!

Best thing about being an Ambassador?
It is an honor to be associated with this impeccable brand, its innovations, and initiatives! CREATE YOUR STYLE with Swarovski Elements is faceted class to the millionth power!

Favorite of the SWAROVSKI ELEMENTS?
Honestly, it changes with each new innovations roll-out. Today, I covet the new crystal pearls Gemcolors (Innovations Spring/Summer 2013). All of them, in every shape, size, and drill!

Inspiration?
The inimitable Alice Korach, founding editor of *Bead & Button* magazine, once said she is sometimes inspired by what she thought she saw. I know exactly what she means. Sometimes I think I see something that stirs my heart! Upon closer inspection, I see something more mundane or predictable by comparison. But I'm left with a glimpse of inspiration that I can execute into an original Brenda Schweder. After all, it's my kooky brain that first flashed the image!

Advice for new beaders?
Play, play, play, then play some more. Allow yourself to be happy with the process, not just the results. I rarely execute the piece that I start out to create—there are just too many way-better iterations along the way!

Surprise Party

Kristal Wick

I made one of these fab dangles for a friend's birthday because they looked like a little present. If one is a present, a whole neck full must be a party! Everybody deserves a splash of sparkle for a birthday; and it's extra special when it's Swarovski. Whether you make these into earrings, a Christmas tree ornament with a single splash, or an entire waterfall, like my necklace, it's a good thing.

materials

SWAROVSKI ELEMENTS

- 6mm 5040 rondelles (58 total):
  - **43** Crystal AB
  - **5** Amethyst Blend
  - **3** Indicolite AB2
  - **3** Caribbean Blue Opal AB2
  - **4** Crystal Copper
- 8mm 5601 cubes (46 total):
  - **8** Amethyst AB
  - **8** Light Sapphire AB
  - **8** Provence Lavender AB
  - **6** Aquamarine AB
  - **7** Caribbean Blue Opal AB
  - **9** Montana AB
- 4mm 5328 bicones (822 total):
  - **49** Montana AB2
  - **49** Antique Pink
  - **49** Light Amethyst AB2
  - **49** Provence Lavender AB
  - **49** Pacific Opal AB2
  - **49** Caribbean Blue Opal AB2
  - **49** Indicolite AB2
  - **49** Amethyst AB2
  - **49** Light Sapphire AB2
  - **49** Erinite AB2
  - **49** Aquamarine
  - **49** Aquamarine AB2
  - **49** Violet AB2
  - **49** Tanzanite AB2
  - **49** Light Azore AB2
  - **31** Air Blue Opal AB2
  - **32** Denim Blue AB2
  - **24** Crystal AB

- 3mm 5328 bicone (86 total):
  - **18** Tanzanite
  - **17** Crystal Copper
  - **17** Amethyst
  - **17** Pacific Opal
  - **17** Indicolite

Other Supplies

- Batik Beauty beads
  - **18** ½ in. small
  - **16** 1 in. medium
  - **9** 1½ in. large
  - **822** 1-in. sterling silver ball-tip headpins
  - **19** 2-in. headpins
- **47** copper flower spacers (TierraCast)
- silver spacers (TierraCast)
  - **133** large
  - **87** small
- eyepins
  - **45** 2 in.
  - **16** 3 in.
  - **9** 4 in.
- clasp
- **2** 6mm jump rings, silver
- **2** crimp tubes, silver
- flexible beading wire .018 silver

Tools

- roundnose pliers
- chainnose pliers
- crimping pliers
- wire cutters

Make Bicone Dangles

1 String a 4mm bicone on a ball-tip headpin and make a plain loop above the beads. Make 822 dangles.

Make Little Presents

2 On a 2-in. headpin, string: small silver spacer, copper spacer, 8mm cube, six bicone dangles, large spacer, 4mm bicone. Make a plain loop above the beads. Make 19 bottom cube presents (**a, left**).

3 On a 2-in. eyepin, string: small silver spacer, copper spacer, 8mm cube, six bicone dangles, large spacer, 4mm bicone. Make a plain loop above the beads. Make 28 middle cube presents (**a, right**).

Make Fabric Bead Links

4 On a 2-in. eyepin, string: 3mm bicone, large spacer, six bicone dangles, 4mm bicone, small Batik Beauty, 4mm bicone, six bicone dangles, large spacer, 3mm bicone. Make 18 small fabric bead links (**b, left**).

5 On a 3-in. eyepin, string: 3mm bicone, large spacer, six 4mm bicone dangles,

a

b

medium Batik Beauty, 4mm bicone, six bicone dangles, large spacer, 3mm bicone. Make a plain loop above the beads. Make 16 medium fabric bead links (**b, middle**).

6 On a 4-in. eyepin, string: 3mm bicone, large spacer, six bicone dangles, 4mm bicone, large Batik Beauty, 4mm bicone, six bicone dangles, large spacer, 3mm bicone. Make a plain loop above the beads. Make nine large fabric links (**b, right**).

7 Make 17 long strands by linking the loops of:
a. Small fabric link, bottom present. Make two.
b. Small fabric link, middle present, small fabric link, bottom present. Make two.
c. Small fabric link, middle present, small fabric link, middle present, small fabric link, bottom present. Make two.
d. Medium fabric link, middle present, small fabric link, middle present, small fabric link, bottom present. Make two.
e. Small fabric link, middle present, medium fabric link, middle present, medium fabric link, bottom present. Make two.
f. Medium fabric link, middle present, medium fabric link, middle present, medium fabric link, bottom present. Make two.
g. Medium fabric link, middle present, medium fabric link, middle present, large fabric link, bottom present. Make two.
h. Medium fabric link, middle present, large fabric link, middle present, large fabric link, bottom present. Make two.
i. Large fabric link, middle present, large fabric link, middle present, large fabric link, bottom present. Make one.

Putting It All Together

8 On beading wire, center a rondelle, a 4mm bicone, strand **i**, a 4mm bicone, and a rondelle.

9 On each end, string a 4mm bicone, strand **h**, a 4mm bicone, and a rondelle. Repeat seven times, substituting strands **g–a** for **h**.

10 On each end, string a 4mm bicone, a bottom present, and a 4mm bicone.

11 On each end, string a rondelle and a small spacer. Repeat 19 times (20 rondelles total), ending with a spacer.

12 On each end, string a 4mm bicone and a crimp tube. Go back through each crimp tube, leaving a small loop of wire. Crimp and trim the excess wire.

13 Attach a clasp half to each end of the necklace with a jump ring.

KRISTAL

Kristal Wick is a frequent guest on PBS, HGTV, and the inventor of Sassy Silkies—handpainted silk beads. Her designs have been featured in over 50 publications. She's authored three best-selling books, including *Fabulous Fabric Beads* and won many international awards including two first place designs in the British Bead Awards competition, first and third place designs in the K. Gottfried Inc. Worldwide Design Contest, finalist in the CHA Indie Craft Contest, finalist at the *Bead & Button* Bead Dreams competition, and third place in the International Design competition sponsored by the Washington D. C. Bead Museum.

KristalWick.com
create-your-style.com/Content.Node/
ambassadors/Kristal-Wick.en.php

"My inspiration changes daily which keeps my work and perspective fresh."

How long have you been making jewelry?
Since my first macaroni necklace, I've enjoyed wearing my own creations. Having spent many years as a technical writer in corporate America having trunk shows in my cubicle, I finally took the leap of faith, followed my dream and haven't looked back! It's been a very bumpy roller coaster ride but worth every white-knuckle moment!

Best advice you've received?
Always use good quality materials and tools for your designs. You never know where they'll end up! From a magazine cover to the dance floor, great quality jewelry withstands the test of time and you won't end up with an inferior end product, breakage, or undesirable surprises.

Favorite tool?
Mini roundnose pliers. I can wire wrap on the plane!

Best thing about being an Ambassador?
EVERYTHING! It's such an honor to be part of the Ambassador family with so many outstanding designers and overwhelming creativity. Tapping into the color trends and shapes of Swarovski Elements has greatly affected my design aesthetic and it's a pleasure to see their new releases before launch time to inform my designs for the coming seasons.

Favorite of the SWAROVSKI ELEMENTS?
The butterfly (5754). Butterflies represent transformation and growth. Add that beautiful Swarovski sparkle and you've got the perfect bead! I try to include them in my designs every chance I get.

Inspiration?
Chocolate, my puppy Sparkle, the majestic Colorado mountains outside my studio and delish java, not necessarily in that order! My inspiration changes daily which keeps my work and perspective fresh.

Advice for new beaders?
Dive in! Fearless Creativity is my motto. There's no such thing as failure in art, you can always slap on another layer to hide the "flaws" and call it mixed media!

Victorian Garden Party

Valeen Hirata

Every design starts with a thought but ends with pure imagination. This necklace started with a color—Fern Green. It was the first box of teardrops I opened, and the beautiful green color winked at me. After I made the sparkling lily flowers, I found a large brass filigree flower and I wired crystal bicones around to make it glisten. The natural choice, then, was to add a mixture of elements to make a chain to pair with my flowers, ending with Victorian Garden Party.

materials

SWAROVSKI ELEMENTS

- **82–85** 5810 8mm round Crystal Pearls, Antique Gold
- 5238 Xilion bicones
    - **5** 6mm Emerald 2X
    - **4** 6mm Fern Green 2X
    - **53** 4mm Dorado 2X
    - **54** 4mm Fern Green AB 2X
    - **4** 4mm Fern Green 2X
    - **5** 3mm Fern Green AB 2X
- 2058 flatback crystals (no hf)
    - **36** 7ss Fern Green
    - 20ss Erinite
- 5000 rounds
    - **12** 8mm Erinite
    - **3** 6mm Palace Green Opal
- 6010 briolette pendants
    - **10** 13x6.6mm Palace Green Opal
    - **26** 11x5.5mm Fern Green

Other Supplies

- 49mm layered filigree flower (Kabela Design)
- 11º seed beads, metallic gold
- **8** leaf bead caps
- **5** fluted bead caps
- **11** eyepins
- **20** headpins
- 40 in. heavy-link chain
- 26-gauge wire
- 40 in. flexible beading wire
- 4 lb. test monofilament
- glue

Sparkling Lilies

1 Using 18 in. of monofilament, string five briolette pendants.

2 Sew back through all petals and tie a knot (**a**), leaving a long tail on each end.

3 With the right end, sew into one briolette. With the left end, pick up seven 11ºs. Cross the right end back through the last two 11ºs (**b**) and tighten.

4 With the right end, sew into the next briolette. With the left end, pick up three 11ºs. Cross the right end through the last two 11ºs and tighten.

5 Repeat step 4 two times.

6 With the right end, sew through the next briolette, and pick up two 11ºs. With the left end, pick up one 11º. Cross the right end through the 11º on the left. Sew through all of the top 11ºs. Tie the ends together in a knot and weave the excess thread through the beads. Cut the thread.

7 Make a total of six five-petal flowers.

8 Repeat steps 1–6 using three briolettes in step 1 and repeating step 4 only one time. Make a total of two three-petal flowers.

Filigree Flower

9 Base layer: Cut a 46-in. piece of 26-gauge wire and attach one end to the outer edge of the base filigree flower. String a 4mm bicone. Bring the wire through the filigree and secure the crystal with a whip stitch (**c**). Repeat around the entire outer edge.

10 Middle layer: With the same piece of wire, sew up through the middle layer and wrap the wire one time around the filigree flower. Sew 4mm bicones onto the filigree petals as you did for the base layer. At each inner "V" between petals, substitute a 3mm bicone.

11 Top layer: Sew up from the bottom so the wire is just outside of the filigree center. String an 8mm round, cross the filigree, and sew back into the filigree. Wrap to secure, and trim any excess wire.

12 Adhere flatback crystals around the center 8mm crystal. Let the glue dry according to the manufacturer's instructions.

a

b

c

Crystal Charms

13 Make 15 charms as pictured (**d**), five of each style.

Flower Tassels

14 Short tassel: On a headpin, string a 6mm bicone, a leaf bead cap, a small five-petal lily, and a fluted beadcap (**e**). Make a plain loop above the beads.

15 Open an eyepin and connect it to the dangle just made. String a 4mm bicone, a large five-petal lily, a fluted beadcap, a small five-petal lily, and a fluted beadcap. Make a plain loop above the beads.

16 Connect the loop to a three-link piece of chain (**f**).

17 Long tassel: On a headpin, string a 6mm bicone, a leaf beadcap, a small five-petal lily, and a leaf beadcap. Make a plain loop above the beads.

18 Open an eyepin and connect it to the dangle just made. String a 5mm bicone, a large five-petal lily, a fluted beadcap, and a leaf beadcap. Make a plain loop above the beads.

19 Open an eyepin and connect it to the dangle just made. String a 6mm bicone, a small five-petal lily, and a fluted beadcap. Make a plain loop above the beads.

20 Connect the loop to a four-link piece of chain.

Necklace Strands
Strand 1

21 On flexible beading wire, string a bicone, a seed bead, and a pearl. String a seed bead, a bicone, a seed bead, and a pearl and repeat three times. String a seed bead and a pearl. Repeat four times.

22 Alternate the patterns in step 20 until the strand is the desired length. String a bicone.

23 String a crimp bead and a seven-link piece of chain. Go back through the crimp bead and a few more beads. Crimp the crimp bead.

24 Repeat step 23 on the other end.

Strand 2

25 On an eyepin, string an 8mm round. Make a plain loop. Make seven round links.

26 On an eyepin, string a pearl, a bicone, a pearl, a bicone, and pearl. Make a plain loop above the beads. Make eight pearl links.

27 Cut 15 three-link pieces of chain.

28 Connect one side of the strand: pearl link, chain, round link, chain, pearl, chain, round, chain, pearl, chain (**g**).

29 Connect the other side of the strand: round link, chain, pearl link, chain, round, chain, pearl, chain, round, chain, pearl, chain, round, chain, pearl, chain, round, chain, pearl, chain.

Strand 3

30 Cut a 26-in. piece of chain.

Connect Everything:

31 Use chain links as jump rings to attach each end of strands 1 and 2 to opposite sides of the filigree (**h**).

32 Open the end links of the long chain and attach to the filigree on opposite sides.

33 On one side, attach tassels to the end links of strands 1 and 2.

34 Link crystal charms and three-petal flowers onto center links on strand 2 (**i**).

Valeen Hirata resides in beautiful sunny Hawaii where there is always cause for inspiration! She is also a two-time award-winning designer in the CREATE YOUR STYLE Design Competition, Professional category. Her designs are made to create and inspire others to try old and new SWAROVSKI ELEMENTS. She also designs kits for the DIY market. Val spends her everyday life in a bead and wedding shop surrounded by sparkle and is a proud mother and grandmother.

www.cbysparkle.com
create-your-style.com/Content.Node/
ambassadors/Valeen-Hirata.en.php

"From the moment I realized that I could actually make jewelry, I was hooked."

How long have you been making jewelry?
From the moment that I realized that I could actually make jewelry, I was hooked! So, my total years of making jewelry is 18, I've been beading for 10 years, and I've been making jewelry that I love for the last six years. From the moment I created my first fabulous piece, I knew this was meant to be.

Best advice you've received?
To create what I love the most.

Favorite tool?
My hands because they're what I use most of all. My other favorite is my roundnose pliers because they're the most versatile.

Best thing about being an Ambassador?
I love that I am surrounded by an amazing group of talented artists along with support of Swarovski. We feed off of each other's talents and knowledge, and we have worldwide exposure. Therefore, we are able to share the sparkle and happiness with others.

Favorite of the SWAROVSKI ELEMENTS?
I love fancy stones simply because they sparkle the most.

Inspiration?
Everything inspires me! Texture, the wind blowing, a color, a memory, etc. My real love is the Victorian era.

Advice for new beaders?
Go with your instinct and don't be afraid to try. Start with a kit using a good product because it gives you a better start to finishing, and will build confidence.

Pink Orbits

Leslie Rogalski

I love weaving SWAROVSKI ELEMENTS on a loom for their sparkle and texture. With the weft threads running straight through the holes, the threads are safe and secure from any possible abrasion. The colors and checkerboard motif in this cuff are inspired a bit from Cirque de Soleil, and a bit from space-age graphics. The focal element uses layers of brick-stitched rubber O-rings—one of my signature components. A spiral wired rubber tube toggle sends the closure spinning in a new dimension.

materials

SWAROVSKI ELEMENTS
- 5000 round
  - **207** 3mm Jet (A)
  - **207** 3mm Crystal (B)
  - **118** 3mm Fuchsia (C)
  - **80** 2mm Jet (D)

Other Supplies
- Beadalon WildFire black .006
- #12 loom beading needles (at least 2 in.)
- #12 1½-in. hard beading needles
- 3-in. hard beading needles
- black rubber O-rings, cross section ³⁄₁₆ in.
  - 20mm OD
  - **2** 12mm OD
  - **3** 10mm OD
  - **2** 8mm OD
- Beadalon ring-sized memory wire, 2 complete coils
- 4 in. 1.7mm hollow rubber tubing, black

Tools
- loom
- roundnose pliers
- chainnose pliers
- memory wire cutters
- scissors for WildFire

Please note: These directions are for a 7-in. bracelet. Add or subtract three rows to lengthen or shorten. Leave six rows of overlap beneath the button hole to accommodate the toggle loops.

Weave the Cuff

1 Warp the loom with eight threads of WildFire for a cuff seven beads wide. Depending on the spacing of your loom's warping coil or screw rod, you may need to warp every other coil to allow for the 3mm crystals. This pattern creates 75 woven rows (7 in.). Leave 5 in. of extra thread at each end of the warp threads for easier finishing.

2 Start with the buttonhole end first and follow the loom graph (**figure 1**). Use the instructions included with the loom for setting up the warp and weaving basics.

3 Thread the loom needle with a comfortable length of thread. Tie a half-hitch knot with the tail onto one side warp thread, leaving enough tail to weave in later. Remember to leave the extra warp length for finishing off.

tip Righties usually knot on the left warp and work by stringing from left to right, and then passing back through the beads from right to left. Lefties may be comfortable knotting on the right warp thread and stringing from right to left, and then passing from left to right.

Rows 1–3
4 With 3mm Jet, Crystal, and Fuchsia rounds (A, B, and C), weave the checkered cuff. To weave a basic row on a loom, with your working thread passing left to right beneath the warp threads, string 3A, 1C, and 3B. Pop them up between the warp threads and hold them in place with your finger. Pass back through the crystals so the working thread now goes over the warp threads, sandwiching the beads in place. Repeat for 3 rows.

Buttonhole
5 Weave rows 4, 5, and 6 in two parts, called split loom. Do not add beads in

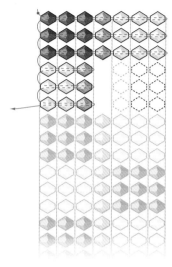

figure 1

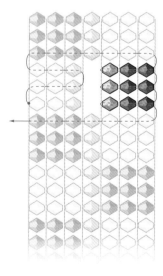

figure 2

the middle of those rows to leave a space between the center warp threads. Weave two Bs and a C on one side of rows 4, 5, and 6 (**figure 1**). Work back through the beads to exit row 3, and weave a C and two As on the other side of rows 4, 5, and 6. Continue with row 7 and on in complete rows (**figure 2**).

figure 3

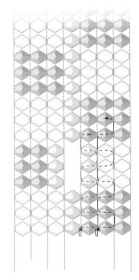

figure 4

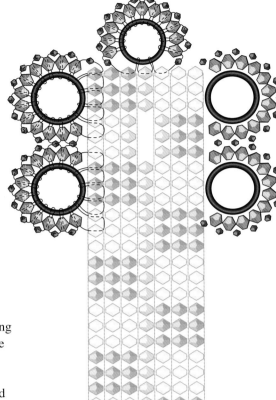

figure 5

Toggle Loops

6 Check the fit of the cuff, overlapping it on your wrist and keeping the buttonhole on top. Note which rows show beneath the buttonhole because that is where you'll attach the toggle loop O-rings. Place two 8mm O-rings side by side. Stitch the O-rings parallel to the middle C stripe along the noted rows. Use a new doubled length of thread. Secure the thread in the beadwork to exit a C. Pass through both O-rings and through the same C, snugging the O-rings to the cuff. Pass through the next C and the O-rings, and through the Cs again. Repeat for a third C, secure the thread in the beadwork so the O-rings are tight to the cuff, and trim (**figure 3**).

Finishing the Warp

7 Cut the cuff from the loom, leaving long warp threads at both ends. One by one, starting from the center warp threads out to each side, thread each tail on a needle and weave in the tail, zigzagging down its own column for several rows. Exit within the beadwork—not along the side—and trim (**figure 4**).

Toggle Spiral Ring

The toggle loops fit up through the buttonhole. The toggle spiral will slip through both rings, holding the closure.

8 Use roundnose pliers to make a very tiny loop in one end of the memory wire.

String a C and the thin rubber tube. String another C. Make another tiny loop in the memory wire. Use a dowel or pen and your fingers to adjust the memory wire into a pleasing spiral by shaping one end of the coil smaller.

Focal Rings

9 Work circular brickstitch using Cs with Ds between. Only the largest O ring is stitched completely around, and then added on top of the cuff.

note The large ring is stitched to the cuff in only three places. The smaller rings are only partially brick-stitched so their unbeaded sections fit alongside the edges of the cuff (**figures 5 and 6**).

Sizes are graduated from three 10mm rings (on the end and adjacent sides), two 12mm rings linked to the 10mm rings (sharing Ds with the 10mm rings) stitched to the sides of the cuff, and the large 20mm positioned on top to slightly overlap the two side 12mm rings but not blocking the button hole.

3mm crystal, color A
3mm crystal, color B
3mm crystal, color C
2mm crystal, color D

black rubber O ring

figure 6

LESLIE

Leslie Rogalski is best known for her unique beadweaving designs. Her acclaimed DOODLEBEADS method of teaching bead stitching has empowered students through DVDs and e-mags, on the PBS TV show Beads, Baubles, and Jewels, and on Jewelry Television. The former editor-in-chief of a popular bead magazine, she is a member of the Beadalon design team, and she designs for many other industry leaders. Leslie's designs and articles on beading have been widely published. It was her honor to be a judge for one of the CREATE YOUR STYLE International Design Competitions.

sleeplessbeader.blogspot.com
sleeplessbeader.com
leslierogalski.com
create-your-style.com/Content.Node/
ambassadors/LESLIE-ROGALSKI.php

"Use the best materials you can afford."

How long have you been making jewelry?

Making jewelry became my real vocation in about 1992. Until then I'd been an illustrator, a writer, and a designer of fiber art and wearable art. I began using beadwork on totem sculptures using a friend's handwoven fabric, and people wanted to wear the adornment on the figures. Things evolved from there. I'd been writing about art and design since high school, so taking a job as editor-in-chief of a jewelry magazine was a giant step along this path and a total affirmation that this is the realm where I belong. I've never looked back.

Best advice you've received?

Do what you love.

Favorite tool?

Good task lamps and magnifier glasses are my most important tools. Those—and a really good pair of scissors.

Best thing about being an Ambassador?

The honor of having my creative style selected to represent a legacy of art and superb craft is second only to the pleasure of being in the company of such fabulous and fun people, including the other designers and Swarovski staff I've met.

Favorite of the SWAROVSKI ELEMENTS?

As a bead stitcher and weaver, I mostly enjoy and employ the round and Xilion beads (upgraded bicone) in many sizes, and crystal pearls. But each new Innovation product lures me!

Inspiration?

My ideas for shape, form, and often color come from insignia and medals of honor, medieval banners, tribal totems, Art Deco and ancient Egyptian motifs, and futuristic industrial design, but materials are my real jumping-off point. I look at the "many" (elements) and then invent the "whole." I am definitely a minimalist and maker of singular components.

Advice for new beaders?

Learn all the techniques you can to have a rich vocabulary at your disposal. Make sure your craft is always the best it can be. Use the best materials you can afford. Take classes from teachers whose style you admire—but never sell or teach ideas from others without their permission. Be as fearless as fiscally possible in building a stash—you can't design freely without enough materials to inspire you. Keep a sketchbook or idea board. Support your local bead shop!

Sparkle Sprockets

Stephanie Dixon

What I really like about this project is that it's convertible—you can wear it so many ways! Do you prefer one sparkle sprocket or nine on the chain? You can even hook them to earring wires for earrings. How about key rings? At the end of a bookmark? I hope that this project is just a starting point as you dive into a crystal pool of sparkle sprockets.

materials

SWAROVSKI ELEMENTS

- **70** 5810 4mm round pearls, Crystal Petrol
- 5328 Xilion bead
  119 4mm Crystal Golden Shadow
  70 4mm Denim Blue
  70 4mm Crystal Bronze Shade
  4 5mm Crystal Bronze Shade
- 6010 Briolette drop
  2 11x5.5mm Crystal Golden Shadow
  2 17x8.5mm Denim Blue
- 6320 crystal rhombus pendant
  27mm Crystal Golden Shadow
  2 19mm Crystal Golden Shadow
  2 14mm Crystal Golden Shadow

Other Supplies

- 20 in. brass oxide chain (Garlan chain style 405X4I)
- 30 yd. spool 22-gauge wire, gunmetal (Parawire)
- hammertone ellipse brass oxide clasp (TierraCast)
- **9** 10mm antique brass lobster claw clasps
- **2** jump rings

Tools

- roundnose pliers
- chainnose pliers
- Coiling Gizmo with large mandrel
- wire cutters

Make a Sparkle Sprocket

1 String 35 4mm Xilion bicone crystals onto the spool of 22-gauge wire.

2 Attach the wire to the Coiling Gizmo and wrap the wire around the mandrel approximately five times.

3 Continue to turn the crank, feeding crystals up the wire as you turn.

4 When all the crystals are used, turn the crank five more times. Cut the wire at each end of the sparkle sprocket.

5 Follow steps 1–4 to create:
3 Crystal Golden Shadow sparkle sprockets
2 Denim Blue sparkle sprockets
2 Crystal Bronze Shade sparkle sprockets
2 Crystal Petrol Pearl sparkle sprockets

6 Carefully trim the ends of the sparkle sprockets from five loops to three. Set aside.

7 Cut nine 4-in. pieces of 22-gauge wire.

8 Using roundnose pliers about 1½ in. from one end of a 4-in. piece of wire, make the first half of a wrapped loop. Connect a 11x5.5mm briolette pendant and complete the wrapped loop. Repeat with the 17x8.5mm briolette pendant, the 14mm rhombus pendant, the 19mm rhombus pendant, and the 27mm rhombus pendant. (For the larger rhombus pendants, create the wrapped loop on the larger part of roundnose pliers so that the pendant will slide easily onto the wrap.)

tip Add the sparkle sprockets to the wire pendant units following my order (see photo) or make this project your own and have fun with your own combinations.

9 On the large rhombus pendant unit, string a 4mm Crystal Golden Shadow bicone, a sparkle sprocket, and a 4mm bicone. Make the first half of a wrapped loop above the beads, connect a lobster claw clasp, and complete the wraps.

10 Repeat with the remaining pendants and sparkle sprockets, following the photo or choosing your own combinations.

11 Attach the hammered ellipse toggle clasp to the chain with jump rings. I used a 20-in. piece of chain, but you may like yours shorter. Attach the sparkle sprocket pendant units to the chain.

STEPHANIE

Stephanie Dixon (aka The Dixon Chick) is a well known designer and teacher specializing in wire techniques. Living in Toronto, Canada, she is one of two Canadian CREATE YOUR STYLE with SWAROVSKI ELEMENTS Ambassadors. An avid crocheter since the age of 9, she started adding beads to her work, and a new addiction was born. Stephanie loves teaching students new techniques and creates pieces that give instant gratification. Some of her recent adventures have been teaching at the gem and mineral shows in Tucson and at the Bead&Button Show, as well as mentoring and teaching on the CREATE YOUR STYLE cruise 2011 and 2013. Stephanie is a proud member of the Toronto Bead Society and the West Toronto Beading Guild.

create-your-style.com/Content.Node/ambassadors/Stephanie-Dixon.en.php

"Life's not about the money—it's about the sparkle!"

How long have you been making jewelry?
I have been making jewelry since 2006 but have been a lover of all crafts since I started crocheting at age 9. I sew, knit, crochet, cross-stitch, and paint. All of these skills are easily translated to jewelry making. I knew this would be my livelihood when my job was getting in the way of my beading. So I quit my corporate job after 22 years and haven't looked back!

Best advice you've received?
"Do what you love and the money will follow." Many people have told me this over the years and I live a happy and stress-free life when I remember to follow this mantra. Life's not about the money—it's about the sparkle!

Favorite tool?
Xuron's Tapered Head Micro-Shear Flush Cutters (Model 9200). I cannot live without these! I have three pairs just in case one goes AWOL.

Best thing about being an Ambassador?
There are so many wonderful things about being an ambassador that it is hard to pick just one! The opportunity to work with and share ideas with an incredibly talented group of people. The opportunity to travel the world on the CREATE YOUR STYLE cruise and meet crystal aficionados from all over. To speak at my son's elementary school at Career Day and introduce SWAROVSKI ELEMENTS to the next generation of beaders. The opportunity to do charitable works such as teaching make-and-takes in hospitals and donating jewelry to programs such as the Corsage Project and Inside the Dream (enabling young women to attend prom who otherwise wouldn't be able to afford it).

Favorite of the SWAROVSKI ELEMENTS?
These are tough questions! I love them all! The Crystal Yarn is a dream to work with. The briolette pendants are so delicate and reflect the light beautifully. The Crystal Pearls pair well with all the other elements. But, my favorite is the bicone, as it's the building block of so many designs.

What inspires you?
First and foremost I am inspired by color: the interplay of unusual combinations. Subtle monochromatic designs. Vibrant oppositional schemes. Color in nature—an endless color palette to draw inspiration from.

Advice for new beaders?
Don't be afraid of color. I keep my bicones in clear round acrylic containers. I can come up with new color combinations easily as I move the containers around on my desk. Try all sorts of different techniques: wirework, seed bead stitching, crochet, kumihimo. You will always learn something and add to your skill set. And of course: You can do it!

Mermaid Song

Laura Timmons

I love the sea. It conjures feelings of peace and tranquility. Water is my therapy. Rich colors of deep blues, greens, and turquoises all beckon us. Mermaids are beautiful, mysterious creatures of the sea, with their enchanting songs, always drawing us closer.

materials

SWAROVSKI ELEMENTS

- 6723 28x28 shell pendant, Crystal AB
- 30mm 6720 3-sprig coral, Crystal
- **3** 18mm 6727 fish pendant, Indicolite
- 25 in. 40415 1445607 round cupchain, Black Diamond
- 5000 round
   - **25** 8mm Sand Opal
   - **25** 8mm Olivine
   - **25** 6mm Aquamarine
- 5328 Xilion bicone
   - **38** 6mm Sahara 2XAB
   - **25** 6mm Olivine AB
   - **28** 8mm Crystal AB
- 5601 cube
   - **24** 8mm Indicolite
   - **26** 8mm Erinite AB
      6mm 5301, Crystal AB 2X

- 6721 Starfish
      40mm Crystal with Verde coating
   - **27** 16mm Indicolite

Additional Supplies

- 150 ft. Parawire 24-gauge wire, Vintage Bronze
- ¾ in. Anna's toggle, color 27, TierraCast
- **2** tall radiant cones, color 27, TierraCast
- **2** 2-in. eyepins, color 27, TierraCast
- 30 in. 12mm WireLace, grass
- E-6000 adhesive

Tools

- Simplicity crochet hook size I
- bentnose pliers
- wire cutters

tips When crocheting, it is not necessary to vary beads on each strand—once you braid your strands together, it creates the varied effect.

Don't worry about stitching perfect crochet chain circles. You will never notice it after the piece is braided. Some of the more unusual and interesting pieces are created with inconsistent chains. Keep consistency in your stitch size (about the size of a large pea) and your gauge will be fine.

To extend the length of your necklace, add beads to the end. If the necklace is longer than you would like, you can gently scrunch the wire to shorten.

Getting Started

You will create nine individual strands of crocheted chain with captured beads, and then braid these strands along with two additional strands together for the necklace. Each of the nine strands will contain 24 of the same bead on each strand.

Prepare the Strands

1 Thread 24 Sand Opal rounds for Strand 1 onto the wire. Leaving 5 in. of wire (the tail) at the beginning, chain one empty chain stitch with your hook and wire. Slide a bead against the last chain, and chain as though the bead isn't there—the bead will capture itself in the center of that chain. Alternate an empty chain and a captured bead until all the beads are used. After you capture the last bead, cut the wire and leave a 5-in. tail. Chain one more time, pulling the wire gently through the last chain (creating an empty chain to finish off your strand).

2 Create strands 2–8 by repeating step 1 eight times with additional bead colors and shapes. Flatten each strand with your fingers. When you are finished with all of the strands, you will have one strand each of Sand Opal 8mm Rounds, Olivine 8mm Rounds, Aquamarine 6mm Rounds, Sahara 2XAB 6mm Xilion, Olivine AB 6mm Xilion, Crystal AB 8mm Xilion, Indicolite 8mm Cubes, and Erinite AB 8mm Cubes.

3 Use round cupchain for strand 10. Cut the cupchain to a length similar to the chain stitch strands from steps 1 and 2 (measure from stitch to stitch). Use wire cutters to cut the cupchain at the small link that connects each cupped crystal.

4 Cut a piece of wire 10 in. longer than the cupchain. Leave a 5-in. tail and wrap the wire around the cupchain between every third or fourth cupped crystal. You are securing the wire along the length of the cupchain and giving it a spine or support for the necklace.

5 Use Wire Lace for the eleventh strand. It is ready for braiding.

Almost There

6 Lay the 10 strands from steps 1–4 neatly together on a flat surface and find the center point of each strand. At the farthest point of chain stitch, twist all the strand ends together. (You may have some empty wires that you will braid with in the beginning—that's OK! They will provide a nice taper at the ends of the necklace.)

7 With the WireLace, tie a slip knot on top of the twist you just created.

8 Separate two groups of four strands and one group of three strands. One of the groups should contain both the cupchain strand and the WireLace so you can manipulate them as you braid the strands together (you want them to be prominent in your necklace). Gently braid the strands to fit nicely against each other; don't braid so tightly as to lose the shape of your chain stitches. Braid until you reach the end chain stitch on the longest strand.

9 Twist the ends together, and with the WireLace, tie a slip knot on top of the twist you just created. Trim any excess. Secure the WireLace with E-6000.

10 Leave out four of the wires and wirewrap the rest around the base of the initial twist. Cut off any excess wire. String the four wires through the cone, and make a wrapped loop, capturing one half of the toggle. Trim the excess wire and use bentnose pliers to smooth the ends. Repeat on the other end of the necklace with the other half of the clasp.

The Finishing Touch

11 For the crystallized wire bail, cut two 15-in. pieces of wire. String both strands through the largest starfish hole, and bend at the center of the wire. Bring the wires together and twist all four wires for ¼ in.

12 String the large shell pendant on the wire, and make another ¼-in. twist.

13 String the three-sprig coral, two fish pendants, and an 8mm Crystal AB Xilion. Make another ¼-in. twist.

14 String a small starfish and an 8mm Light Grey Opal Round. Make another ¼-in. twist.

15 String a fish pendant and an 8mm Crystal AB Xilion. Make another ¼-in. twist.

16 Split the wires. String six 6mm Sahara 2XAB over two wires and repeat with the remaining two wires (this is the back of the bail).

17 Fold the piece in half (with the Sahara 2XAB at the back). Wrap the bail around the center of the necklace. Take the wire (at the bottom of the bail now), and wrap around the wire at the top of the large starfish a couple of times to secure.

Embellish the Ends of the Wires

18 Wire 1: String an 8mm Crystal AB Xilion, a 6mm Sahara 2XAB, and a small starfish, *trim the wire ¼ in. and create a little curly loop at the end*. **Wire 2**: String an 8mm Round Olivine, an 8mm Erinite AB Cube, and a 6mm Sahara 2XAB, and repeat from * to * above. **Wire 3:** String a 8mm Crystal AB Xilion, a 6mm Olivine AB, and a 6mm Crystal 2XAB, and repeat from * to * above. **Wire 4**: String an 8mm Erinite AB Cube, a 6mm Aquamarine Round, and a small starfish, and repeat from * to * above. Your final embellishments will lie on top of the large starfish. Whoop! Whoop! You are done, girl!

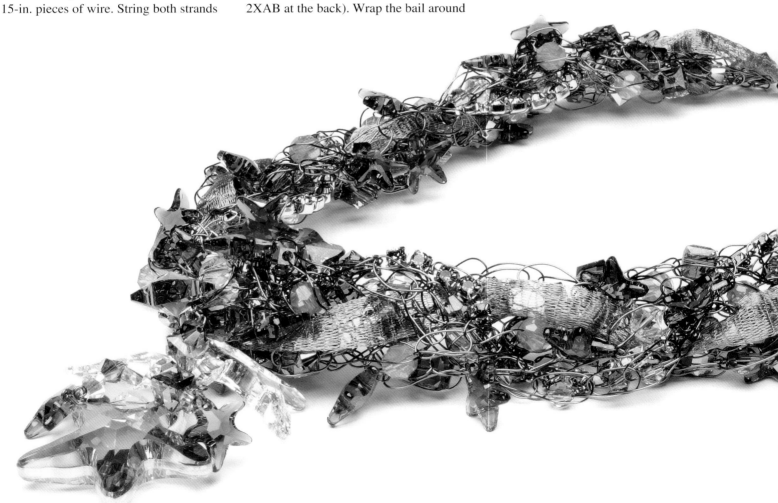

Laura R. Timmons has been designing and teaching professionally for the past eight years. As an Ambassador for CREATE YOUR STYLE with SWAROVSKI ELEMENTS, she has traveled the world extensively, teaching for International Swarovski offices and CREATE YOUR STYLE Partners. Laura is also the fashion editor for Bead Design Magazine, bringing the fashion industry to the beading industry with her "Beading and Fashion 411." Laura has been published in many magazines and has won national competitions with her crochet wire designs.

vintagemoon.net.
create-your-style.com/Content.Node/ambassadors/Laura-Timmons.en.php

"Find three techniques that you like and refine those."

How long have you been making jewelry?
Well, I have been designing since I was a little girl; my mom and grandmother always had my hands working on something. My bachelor's degree is in fashion design. It wasn't until about eight years ago, when I taught my first class, that I realized that this was my true passion. The students' yearn for more kind of fuels the fire, and adds great inspiration to my next designs!

Best advice you've received?
Never, ever question the value of a project, design, or piece. Always believe in yourself and that you are worthy of success.

Favorite tool?
Well, my first response would be my hands. No matter where I am teaching in the world, or what language barriers we have, hands are the true universal language. The second of course would my crochet hook—I always have one on me! You never know when an opportunity to create may arise.

Best thing about being an Ambassador?
Swarovski bar none stands way above all others in the design industry—always stepping up a notch with new colors and shapes. Their fashion forecasting is just brilliant, and is such an amazing aid to any designer. Who wouldn't want to represent an amazing company like this?

Favorite of the SWAROVSKI ELEMENTS?
I would have to say the Cosmic Ring. Although it has been around for a few years, its beauty and versatility stand alone. I find myself using it in so many designs. Plus it actually fits my ring finger—need I say more?

Inspiration?
Everything! From a brilliant orange, ocher-colored sunrise on the beach to the rich purple hues of a sunset in the mountains. An aging brick wall. A Christmas tree. We can find inspiration in everything if we just breathe every once in awhile and soak in the moment.

Advice for new beaders?
Believe in yourself! Never underestimate your worth, whether you are starting a new business selling jewelry or just having fun. Find three techniques that you really like, and refine those. Sometimes when we start in so many different directions, we feel like we have never really accomplished anything.

Blooming
Earrings

Lilian Chen

My wire earring process is simple: I make it easy to finish identical pieces without repeating, wire wrapping, measuring, or soldering. Work with my unique sculpting method, shape connection, and bead and color combinations for a finished piece that is bright and eye-catching. I always leave the finishing for you to do on your own. Be creative and original!

Lilian's Wire Method

1 In the **horizontal gripping position (a)**, hold the pliers and the wire coil parallel to the table. Turn the pliers to create a 90-degree bend, resulting in a three-dimensional shape **(b)**.

2 In the **vertical gripping position (c)**, hold the pliers parallel and the wire perpendicular to the table. Turn the pliers inward to create a 45-degree bend, resulting in a two-dimensional shape with the wire ends following the natural curve and coming together (like a leaf) **(d)**. Leading the wire in the opposite direction from the starting point **(c)** changes the curve **(e)** and directs the ends away from each other.

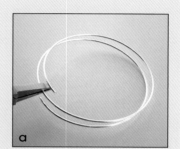

a

b

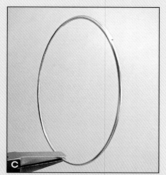

c

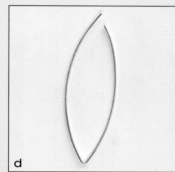

d

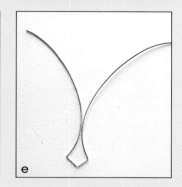

e

First, we'll practice the horizontal and vertical working movements by making a single piece (without beads) with a two-dimensional ribbon shape.

Two-dimensional Ribbon Shape

1 Cut two circles from the 16-gauge wire spool **(f)**.

2 Gripping the end, pull the wire gently to increase the size of the circle **(g)**. This is similar to straightening, but the wire will still have its curve.

3 Make a vertical movement: Grip the wire with your fingers as described in the "vertical gripping position," and push the point with your thumb to form the curve of the first ribbon **(h)**. Push both ends to cross in a ribbon shape. Adjust the shape and size as you wish.

4 Grip one piece of wire with flatnose pliers in the horizontal position at the crossing point **(i)**.

5 Turn your wrist and bend the wire toward you in a 180-degree motion as if you are folding the wire **(j)**, finishing with the tail crossing the first ribbon in the middle and parallel to the edges **(k)**.

tip If the working wire crosses, practice the motion in step 5.

6 Form the second ribbon as in step 3 **(l–n)**. Bring the wire tail from the second ribbon through the bend in the first ribbon. Adjust as desired.

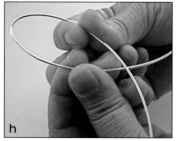

f

g

h

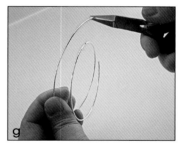

i

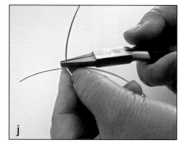

j

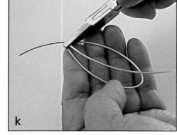

k

l

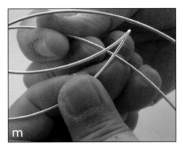
m

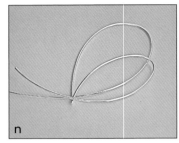
n

A Pair of Identical Blooming Earrings

This pair-making method repeats the same working process as in the single piece, but you will work with two pieces of wire together as one, add the crystals, and finish an identical pair of earrings simultaneously without measuring or repeating.

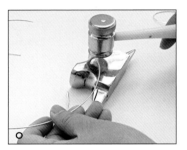
o

p

q

r

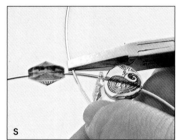
s

t

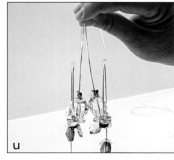
u

1 Cut two sets of circles from the wire spool as in step 1 of the Two-dimensional Ribbon Shape.

2 Gripping both wire ends, gently pull to increase the circle as in step 2 of the Two-dimensional Ribbon Shape.

3 Hammer the ends (**o**) in the horizontal position. Trim the wires to the same length.

4 String a heart bead, a baroque, a twist, a heart pendant, and a rivoli pendant on each wire (**p**).

5 Separate the beads between the twist and the heart pendant as shown (**q**), and tape the two pieces of wire together.

6 Repeat step 3 of the Two-dimensional Ribbon Shape (with two pieces of wire). See (**r**) for the first ribbon shape.

7 With flatnose pliers in the horizontal position, grip one side of the wire at the cross point (note the position of the heart bead and the baroque pendant) (**s**), and repeat the process as in step 5 of the Two-dimensional Ribbon Shape.

8 Add a baroque, a rivoli, a lucerna, and a butterfly to each second ribbon shape (**t**).

9 Grip the two pieces of wire as one at the center of the ribbons in the vertical position (**u**). Repeat the process in step 3 of the Two-dimensional Ribbon Shape (**v**).

10 Cross the wire end over the first ribbon, and lock the end in the bend made in step 7.

11 On the final side add a baroque, a fish, and a heart pendant. Attach an earring wire to each earring (**w**).

materials
SWAROVSKI ELEMENTS
- **2** 18mm 5030 lucerna, Crystal Golden Shadow
- 16x11mm 6090 baroque pendant,
    - **2** Light Amethyst
    - **2** Ruby
    - **2** Crystal AB
- **2** 14mm 5742 heart bead, Crystal Red Magma
- **2** 14mm 5621 twist, Paisley
- **2** 14mm 5727 fish, Crystal Silver Night
- 10.3x10mm 6228 heart pendant
    - **2** Amethyst Blend
    - **2** Crystal Silver Shade
- 8mm 6428 rivoli pendant
    - **2** Fern Green
    - **2** Chrysolite Opal
- **2** 5mm 5754 butterfly, Fern Green

Other Supplies
- spool 16-gauge German style wire, silver
- pair of earring wires, silver

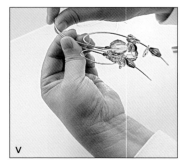
v

w

LILIAN

Lilian Chen is an internationally known wire and bead artist from California. Awards include those from CREATE YOUR STYLE: Be Naturally Inspired USA 2008, Bead&Button Show's Bead Dreams 2008, and Fire Mountain Gems and Beads 2011. Her designs have been featured in beading and wire magazines, including the CREATE YOUR STYLE with SWAROVSKI ELEMENTS 2011 Water magazine. She was the 2012 designer of the year for *Step by Step Wire Jewelry*. Lilian shares her work with students and fans worldwide through her Facebook page and the CREATE YOUR STYLE with SWAROVSKI ELEMENTS sparkling community website, and would love to hear from anyone who has questions about her projects. Teaching venues include Bead&Button, CREATE YOUR STYLE with SWAROVSKI ELEMENTS in Tucson, Crystal Chix Cruise, and the CREATE YOUR STYLE ANCHORS AWAY Cruise.

facebook.com/goldgatsbydesign
create-your-style.com/Content.Node/
ambassadors/Lilian-Chen.en.php

> "Practice is the key word; mistakes are the way to bring out your design talent."

How long have you been making jewelry?
I have been making jewelry for about seven years. I'm self-taught through working at a local bead store. I knew it would be my livelihood when I officially became an Ambassador to the team of CREATE YOUR STYLE with SWAROVSKI ELEMENTS in 2009.

Best advice you've received?
Someone suggested submitting my work to a magazine when I was working at the store five years ago.

Favorite tool?
Pliers are my best friends. They are essential to my wire designs and for my artwork of forming shapes.

Best thing about being an Ambassador?
For me, the best is being trained as a leader to represent the SWAROVSKI ELEMENTS innovation every season, to work with the interesting new shapes and colors, and to work with a variety of new products to create the most interesting designs.

Favorite of the SWAROVSKI ELEMENTS?
6620 Red Magma 40mm is my favorite piece to use with shining silver or royal gold wire; the finished piece is really bright as fire to catch the eye.

Inspiration?
It could be anything from walking to shopping to just watching something on television—anything in that specific moment. Images start to form and my design is created.

Advice for new beaders?
Practice is the key word; mistakes are the way to bring out your design talent. Combine your skills with others' new products, find new techniques to stand out, and you'll find your unique design style.

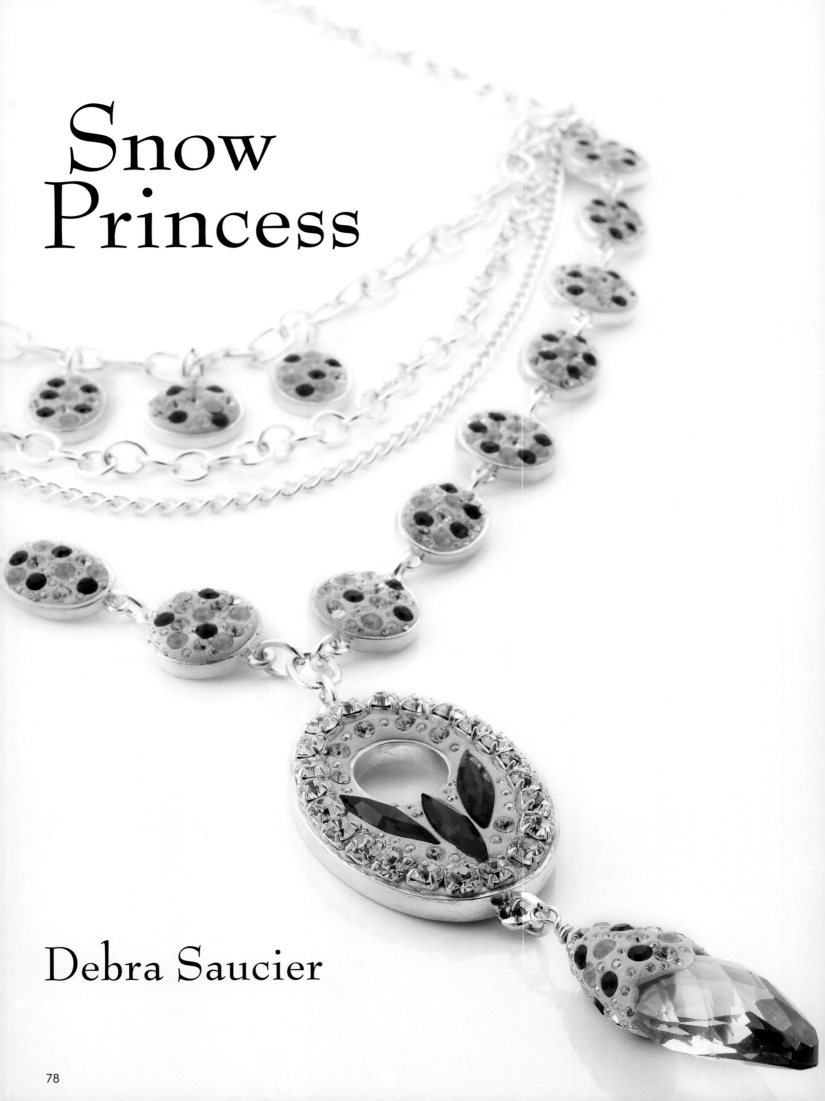

Snow Princess

Debra Saucier

My favorite scenic pictures include a snowcapped Mount Fuji with the bright red contrast of a shrine, taken in Japan near my grandmother's house. Fittingly, my grandmother's name was Yuki, which means snow in Japanese. This necklace is created using mainly Crystal Clay Epoxy Resin Clay and SWAROVSKI ELEMENTS chatons. I love this technique because it allows me to "paint" with Swarovski.

materials

SWAROVSKI ELEMENTS
- **3** 15x4mm 4200 navette, Siam
- 30x14mm 6110 teardrop pendant, Crystal Silver Shade
- **22** chaton montees, Crystal
- **1028 Chaton**
    - **244** pp21 Siam
    - **244** pp21 Silk
    - **244** pp21 Sand Opal
    - **244** pp10 Crystal

Other Supplies
- large oval bezel pendant with two loops
- **8** small-diameter circle bezel charms with two loops
- **6** small-diameter oval bezel charms with two loops
- **2** small-diameter oval bezel charms with one loop
- **2** small-diameter circle bezel charms with one loop
- 22 in. silver-colored garlan chain
- 9 in. silver-colored small-link chain
- 9 in. silver-colored round-link chain
- 22-gauge sterling silver wire
- Crystal Clay Epoxy Resin Clay
- pearl mica powder
- **28** 5mm jump rings
- lobster claw clasp

Tools
- roundnose pliers
- chainnose pliers
- flush wire cutters
- vinyl gloves
- toothpick with beeswax tip
- soft-bristle brush

Small Round and Oval Bezels

Mix the Epoxy Clay
1 Take equal parts of A and B of the epoxy clay. Knead them together until they are no longer marbled. (Working time is approximately 40 minutes to one hour after mixed.)

Mold the Clay into the Bezels
2 Roll the clay into the shape of the bezel setting. If you are using a round bezel, roll the clay into a round ball. Gently pat down the clay so that it is pushed outward and into the edges of the bezel.

Apply the Embellishments
3 Use a beeswax-tipped toothpick to pick up chatons and place them into the clay, foil side down. Place larger chatons first, and then continue with smaller chatons to fill the empty spaces. Once all of the chatons have been placed, brush the entire piece with white pearl mica powder using a soft-bristled brush.

4 Repeat steps 2 and 3 with all the round and oval bezels. Cure for 12–24 hours. Rinse under warm water to remove any additional mica powder or beeswax.

Navette Pendant
5 Cut a 6-in. piece of 22-gauge wire. String the pendant, center it on the wire, and wrap the ends together at the top of the pendant to secure it. Leave one wire end to allow you to make a wrapped loop later after the clay is applied. Trim the remaining wire tail (**a**).

6 Place a piece of mixed epoxy clay around the top of the pendant, covering the base of the twisted wires. Embellish the clay with chatons as in step 3 (**b**).

7 Once all of the chatons have been placed, brush the entire piece with white pearl mica powder using a soft-bristle brush. Cure for 12 to 24 hours. Rinse under warm water to remove any additional mica powder or beeswax.

Large Oval Bezel Pendant

8 Place a piece of mixed epoxy clay into the oval bezel setting. Gently pat down the clay so that it is pushed outward into the edges of the bezel.

9 Embellish the clay with chaton montees around the outer edge (**c**). Place larger chatons and then smaller chatons to fill in the empty spaces. Brush the entire piece with white pearl mica powder using a soft-bristled brush. Cure for 12 to 24 hours. Rinse under warm water to remove any additional mica powder or beeswax.

Necklace Assembly

10 Make a wrapped loop at the top of the navette pendant. Use a jump ring to attach it to the bottom of the large oval bezel. Cut a single link of chain, and use a jump ring to connect the link to the top of the bezel.

11 Using jump rings, attach four two-loop oval bezels and three two-loop circle bezels to form a chain. Repeat with the remaining bezels to form a second chain. Attach one end of each chain to the link at the top of the large oval bezel.

12 Attach one end of the bezel chain to a 22-in. piece of chain approximately 5 in. from the end. Attach the other end of the bezel chain approximately 9 in. from the other chain end. Attach the 9-in. chain pieces to the main chain in the same location as the bezel chain. Attach two single-loop oval and one single-loop circle charms to the center of the main chain.

13 With a jump ring, attach a lobster claw clasp the end of the necklace with the shorter chain. Attach the remaining circle charm to the other end to create a 2½-in. extension.

Debra Saucier is a mixed-media artist who has been beading since summers spent with her grandmother in Japan as a child. Debra was named one of the initial CREATE YOUR STYLE with SWAROVSKI ELEMENTS Ambassadors early in 2009 and has taught at the CREATE YOUR STYLE in Tucson events as well as other shows across the country, including the Bead&Button Show. In 2006, Debra and her husband opened a small bead store called The Bead & Wire Shop. In 2011, Debra launched a new product called Crystal Clay two-part epoxy clay. Her work was recently featured in *Beading Across America*, available from Kalmbach Books.

debrasaucier.com
create-your-style.com/Content.Node/
ambassadors/Debra-Saucier.en.php

"I like the challenge of creating with a stone that has no hole."

How long have you been making jewelry?
I have been making jewelry on and off since I was a child. I started making jewelry seriously about 10 years ago and made it my livelihood 6 years ago.

Best advice you've received?
Don't stress about a project, no matter what it is intended for. Enjoy the process of creativity and the rest will follow.

Favorite tool?
Wire looping pliers are my favorite: The kind with a round nose on one side and a narrow concave second side.

Best thing about being an Ambassador?
It an absolute honor to be counted amongst this most talented group of people. I love the creative sparkling energy that is created when we all get together. It has allowed me to meet some of the most fabulous crafters and hopefully inspired them to sparkle something in their life.

Favorite of the SWAROVSKI ELEMENTS?
I love fancy stones and chatons. I like the challenge of creating with a stone that has no hole.

Inspiration?
Nature inspires me. If we really stop to take a look around us, we can see such a wonderful color palette in nature. The beautiful colors of the New England fall foliage are my favorite.

Advice for new beaders?
Try everything once. There are so many mediums to choose from in jewelry making. Just because you don't like chain mail or stitching, try resin or wireworking.

Mandala of
Glamour

Fernando
DaSilva

My desire was to create a neckpiece that would identify my strong design aesthetic. Purple velvet is one of my favorite colors among the SWAROVSKI ELEMENTS family, and I decided to frame it with rose gold to bring warmth and opulence. The large, fabulous, sew-on stones add fantastic volume, texture, and movement—fundamental qualities for good design.

materials

SWAROVSKI ELEMENTS
- **80** 13x6.5mm 6010 briolette pendant, Tanzanite
- 5328 Xilion beads
  - **21** 2.5mm Crystal Silver Shade
  - **21** 2.5mm Jet Crystal S
  - **21** 2.5mm Tanzanite
  - **27** 6mm Tanzanite
  - **12** 6mm Purple Velvet
  - **15** 7mm Jet Hematite
  - **10** 8mm Tanzanite
  - **29** 8mm Purple Velvet
  - **9** 10mm Purple Velvet
- **11** 16mm 5005 chessboard bead, Crystal Antique Pink
- 3251 sew-on stone
  - **10** 30x15mm Antique Pink
- 1028 round stones
  - **12** pp31 Crystal Vintage Pink
  - **25** pp24 Crystal Vintage Pink
  - **35** pp21 Crystal Vintage Pink
  - **30** pp18 Crystal Vintage Pink

Supplies
- **80** 8º Delicas, steel
- **5** 4-in. medium curb chain pre-made tassels
- **20** rhodium-plated textured bead caps
- **20** copper crimp tubes
- Antique silver extra-large decorated headpin
- **51** 1½-in. rhodium-plated ball-tip headpins
- **45** 8mm rose gold-plated jump rings
- lobster claw clasp, rose gold–plated

- 3 ft. chain, round link and flat connector, rose gold-plated over brass
- 2½ in. oval cable chain, rose gold-plated over brass
- 20 ft. 18-gauge Artistic Wire, dark blue
- 2 ft. Beadalon 49 strands .024 silver-plated flexible beading wire
- spool of 1.0mm Elasticity stretch bead cord, clear
- G-S Hypo Cement

Two-part epoxy clay (DeCoRe):
- **10g** Purple Velvet
- **10g** Tanzanite

Tools
- roundnose pliers
- flatnose pliers
- nylon-jaw pliers
- flush cutters
- toothpick or any round wood stick
- beeswax
- waxed paper
- spatula or knife to cut clay

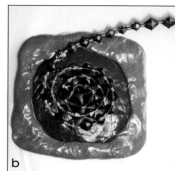

Create the Encrusted Mandala

1 String crimp tube on beading wire and flatten with chainnose pliers. String: 21 2.5mm Crystal Silver Shade beads, crimp tube, 21 2.5mm Jet beads, crimp, 21 2.5mm Tanzanite beads, crimp, six 6mm Tanzanite, crimp, six 8mm Purple Velvet, crimp, six 6mm Purple Velvet, crimp, 6mm Tanzanite, crimp, 7mm Jet Hematite, crimp, 6mm Tanzanite, crimp, 7mm Jet Hematite, crimp, 6mm Tanzanite, crimp, 7mm Jet Hematite, crimp, 6mm Tanzanite, crimp, 7mm Jet Hematite, crimp, six 6mm Purple Velvet, crimp, six 6mm Tanzanite, crimp, six 6mm Purple Velvet, crimp, 7mm Jet Hematite, crimp, three 8mm Purple Velvet, crimp, 6mm Tanzanite, crimp. Flatten the end crimp tube and trim the excess wire.

2 Follow the package instructions to prepare 10g of Tanzanite and 10g of Purple Velvet two-part epoxy clay.

3 Cover a flat surface with waxed paper. Form the Purple Velvet clay into a flat circle. Keep it as round as possible.

4 Form a square frame with the Tanzanite clay around the Purple Velvet circle to create a 2¾x2½-in. shape **(a)**.

5 Gently press the end of the beaded strand (with the larger beads) into the center of the Purple Velvet clay and start forming a spiral, pushing the strand into the epoxy as you go. Make sure the beads are sitting on the side edges **(b)**. Continue spiraling the strand until the entire strand is pushed into the epoxy.

6 Trim the edges of the mandala with a spatula or a knife. Cut the corners on the diagonal to create an octagon-like shape **(c)**.

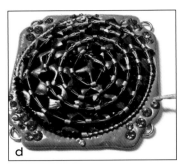

d

e

f

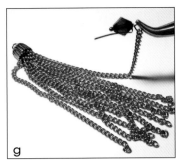

g

h

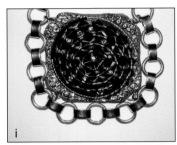

i

7 Set round stones into the Tanzanite frame: Place three pp31 stones on each of the beveled corners. Place a pp24 stone followed by a few pp21 stones to fill in the space on the diagonal. Continue to fill in empty spaces between the large stones around the circle with pp18 stones. Add stones between the bicone beads on the beaded strand for an extra dazzling effect. Create a luscious surface around the circle by randomly placing crystal chatons (**d**).

8 Insert an 8mm jump ring into each corner, leaving half of the ring exposed (**e**). Cure the clay for 24 hours and then peel the waxed paper from the back.

Make the Necklace Components

9 Beaded circles: Cut a 6-in. piece of stretch cord and string a steel Delica bead and a Tanzanite briolette. Alternate the beads until you have four of each strung. Pull the ends tight and tie a double knot (be sure the cord is stretched to the max). Make a single knot on top of the double knot and dab with glue. Put aside and let dry. Make 20 beaded circles.

10 Double beaded links: Cut a 6-in. piece of 18-gauge wire and make a double loop 1½ in. from an end. Wrap the wire two full turns around the base of loop and trim the tail. String: a bead cap, a beaded circle from step 9, a chessboard bead, a beaded circle, and a bead cap. Make a double-wrapped loop above the beads (**f**). Make 10 double beaded links.

11 Beaded tassels: String an 8mm Purple Velvet crystal bead on a ball-tip headpin. Make the first half of a wrapped loop above the bead. Connect an end link of chain and complete the wrapped loop. Repeat on each of the 10 tassel chains. Set aside (**g**).

12 Repeat step 11 with two tassels, substituting five 8mm Tanzanite and five 8mm Purple Velvet beads on each.

13 Repeat step 11 with two tassels, substituting five 6mm Tanzanite and five 7mm Purple Velvet beads on each. Set all the tassels aside.

Assemble the Necklace

14 Follow the pattern (**h**) (begin at the bottom) to connect five long strands: tassel, jump ring, double link, two jump rings, 30x15mm sew-on stone, two jump rings, double link, two jump rings.

15 Cut a 30-in. piece of chain. Frame the mandala (horizontal position) with 11 round textured links in the center of the chain. With a jump ring, connect a round link to each corner of the mandala (**i**).

16 Remove five flat rings from the discarded chain piece. Use a flat ring to attach a sew-on stone to each round link at the bottom of the mandala.

17 Connect each long strand from step 14 to a sew-on stone with two jump rings.

18 Check the fit and trim the chain if necessary. Attach a lobster claw clasp to an end link with a jump ring.

19 String a chessboard bead onto a ball-tip headpin, make the first half of a wrapped loop, and connect it to an end link of the oval plated chain. Complete the wraps and trim the excess wire. Connect the extender to the necklace with a jump ring for an extra touch of glamour.

Necklace is 18 in. long with a 2½-in. extension chain.

FERNANDO

Fernando DaSilva is a jewelry designer, a published author, an instructor, and an avid chef. His work is focused on design and style as key elements of individual expression. He has created jewelry collections for Touchstone Crystal and is a member of the Beadalon Design Team. His work has appeared in *Women's Wear Daily* and *Harper's Bazaar*. He recently designed a line of jewelry components in partnership with John Bead Corp. inspired by Italian architecture, called Instant Glam by Fernando.

dasilvajewelry.com
create-your-style.com/Content.Node/
ambassadors/FERNANDO-DASILVA.en.php

"I had no idea jewelry making would be on my path."

How long have you been making jewelry?
I've been making jewelry for the last 10 years, but I had no idea jewelry making would be on my path.

Best advice you've received?
My mentor taught me to push limits, but most important of all have fun when designing. "It's just jewelry, it's not brain surgery."

Favorite tool?
I don't have a favorite tool because I use many different ones. I thank the divine every day of my life for having my hands to hold tools of work and a healthy mind to search inspiration to refresh my ideas constantly.

Best thing about being an Ambassador?
Having one of the most luxurious brands in the world endorsing my design endeavors—I feel like I belong to a VIP club of very talented artists.

Favorite of the SWAROVSKI ELEMENTS?
It's impossible to pick one favorite element among a wide variety of beauties. I'd rather to say that I move towards the latest and hottest shapes of beads, pendants, and stones because I like the constant transformation of its facets.

Inspiration?
Many different things inspire me, and they are not necessarily all connected to each other. Music in general is an endless source of inspiration; female vocalists always inspire me, especially the work of Brazilian singer Gal Costa; and strong female characters. That, linked with a genuine desire of building a better future, is my inspiration.

Advice for new beaders?
Think outside of the box and do not limit yourself to doing only one thing. Be versatile, learn how to create for yourself, and how to create to please a customer.

Medieval Elegance

Kim St. Jean

I'm an avid reader, and books influence my designs. This necklace was inspired by a story of kings, queens, knights, and dragons. The stone's asymmetrical cut reminded me of a raw stone that would have been found in a mystical cave guarded by a dragon. Setting the stone in a shield fosters the feeling that it has uncontainable power. Joining the copper and silver with cold connections is a technique authentic to the medieval period.

materials

SWAROVSKI ELEMENTS

- 28mm 4759 cosmic flat-back crystal
- **16** 4mm 2400 square flat-back crystals

Other supplies

- 24-gauge copper sheet
- 24-gauge nickel sheet
- G-S Hypo Cement
- **37** 9mm jump rings
- S-hook clasp
- liver of sulfur
- Novacan Black patina
- 0000 steel wool

Tools

- jeweler's saw
- 3/0 saw blades
- V-slot bench pin
- beeswax
- texture hammer
- bench block
- metal shears
- 1.8mm hole-punching pliers
- sanding sponges
- roundnose pliers
- flatnose pliers
- toothpick
- cotton swab
- sandbag or other soft hammering surface
- small ball-peen hammer
- fine-tip permanent marker
- acetone

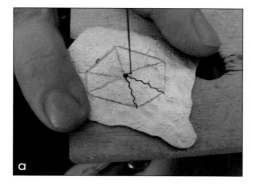

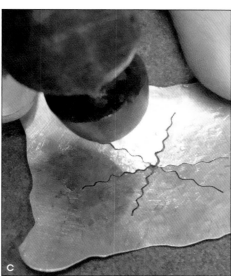

Make the Pendant

1 Texture the nickel sheet as desired.

2 Draw a shield shape on the nickel.

3 Using a jeweler's saw, cut the shield shape from the metal. Sand thoroughly.

4 Place the cosmic fancy crystal in the center of the shield and trace around it.

5 Draw lines from the center to each corner of the shape.

6 Punch a small hole in the center of the traced shape. Thread the saw blade up through the hole and begin sawing curving lines outward from the hole to the corners, loosely following your lines **(a)**.

7 Draw a larger shield shape with prongs on the copper sheet.

8 Using the jeweler's saw, cut out the copper shield. Make sure that you cut each prong at least ¹⁄₁₆-in. past the outer edge.

9 Remove the marks with acetone, and sand the copper shield thoroughly.

10 Lightly texture the front edges and the backs of the prongs **(b)**.

11 Dip the copper component in a warm liver of sulfur solution to add patina. Remove excess patina with 0000 steel wool.

12 Punch a 1.8mm hole in each side of the copper component for the chain connection.

13 Cover the nickel component with Novacan Black using a cotton swab to add patina. Remove excess patina with 0000 steel wool.

14 Place the nickel component on a sandbag or other soft surface, face down. Using the round end of a small ball-peen hammer, gently dap the center of the shield **(c)**. Tap down the edges, leaving the center slightly domed.

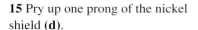

15 Pry up one prong of the nickel shield (**d**).

16 Use roundnose pliers to bend the prong all the way back (**e**). Repeat with the remaining prongs (**f**).

17 Place the crystal in the center of the copper base and place the nickel shield over the crystal. Push each copper prong up over the nickel shield, alternating on opposite sides of the crystal until all of the prongs have been pushed up (**g**).

18 Gently pinch the base of each copper prong with flatnose pliers. Use roundnose pliers to curl the copper prongs up and over the nickel shield (**h**). Use roundnose pliers to ruffle the edges if desired (**i**).

Make the Accents

19 Use metal shears to cut out eight asymmetrical hexagons, each approximately 10x20mm (**j**).

20 Texture both sides of each hexagon. Sand each piece.

21 Punch a 1.8mm hole in the top and bottom of each piece.

22 Add patina with Novacan Black using a cotton swab. Remove excess patina with 0000 steel wool.

23 Place a 4mm ball of beeswax on the tip of a toothpick.

24 Put a small drop of glue on the center of one of the hexagons.

25 Pick up a crystal using the wax end of the toothpick and place it on the dot of glue (**k**).

26 Repeat with each hexagon on both the front and the back.

Assemble the Necklace

27 Using flatnose pliers, connect the jump rings, the pendant, and the hexagon accents. Place three linked jump rings between each accent component.

28 Connect jump rings to finish the chain to the desired length.

29 Attach an S-hook on end link of chain.

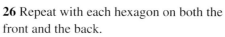

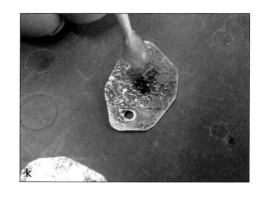

A former public school teacher, **Kim St. Jean** now combines her love of teaching with her creative talent as a jewelry maker. Kim teaches metalworking and other jewelry-making techniques at the William Holland School of Lapidary Arts, John C. Campbell Folk School, the Bead&Button Show, Swarovski's Create Your Style in Tucson, the Wildacres Retreat, and other national venues. When she's not traveling, Kim also teaches at her studio in Myrtle Beach, S. C. Kim has been published in numerous magazines and books, and she has appeared on several beading and craft television programs. Kim is the author of *Mixed Metal Mania: Solder, Rivet, Hammer, and Wire Exceptional Jewelry* and *Metal Magic: How to Etch, Pierce, Enamel, and Set Striking Jewelry*.

kimstjean.com
create-your-style.com/Content.Node/
ambassadors/Kim-StJean.php

"Making jewelry makes me very happy."

How long have you been making jewelry?
I began making macramé jewelry and rings out of colorful telephone wire when I was seven years old. I would go door to door selling them to our neighbors. My mother would call them and tell them I was on my way. They would buy it and she would pay them back. Jewelry became my livelihood in 1998. I quit my job as a public school teacher and opened up my first bead store and boutique. By 2000, my husband, Norm, and I knew that this was what we wanted to do. He quit his high-powered job to join me in my dream. We now live a little more modestly, but we are loving life!

Best advice you've received?
When I quit my job as a public school teacher, my mom told me to do what makes me happy. Making jewelry makes me very happy.

Favorite tool?
Wow, can I pick only one? I guess it's my hammer. But then I'd need my anvil, then my saw, then my bench pin, then my shears …

Best thing about being an Ambassador?
Belonging! I love being a part of such a great group of designers. We are all so diverse. I'm very proud of being able to tell people that I am a CREATE YOUR STYLE with SWAROVSKI ELEMENTS Ambassador.

Favorite of the SWAROVSKI ELEMENTS?
The flatback, round stones, and fancy stones. I love incorporating the perfectly cut stones with my organic, imperfect metal work. I love the "diamonds in the rough" effect—it's unexpected.

Inspiration?
Shape and texture.

Advice for new beaders?
Do what you love. Let the colors, shapes, and textures talk to you and just go with it.

Two By Two

Marcia DeCoster

The Two by Two bracelet uses two rows of diamond lace medallions, which are studded at each corner with Xilion crystals. The center intersection of diamonds is further adorned with an assortment of SWAROVSKI ELEMENTS, which dangle gracefully along your wrist for a major impact of sparkle and swing.

materials

SWAROVSKI ELEMENTS

- **20** 3mm pearl, Antique Bronze (D)
- **91** 4mm 5328 bicone, Emerald AB 2X (E)
- **21** 4mm 3128 lochrosen (F)
- **5** 14 mm 6320 rhombus, Golden Shadow
- **10** 12mm 5523 cosmic bead, Indicolite
- **5** 14x10 5050 oval bead, Golden Shadow

Other supplies

- < .5g 15º seed beads, bronze (A)
- 2g 11º seed beads, green (B)
- 10g 8º seed beads, bronze (C)
- **5** 4mm jump rings
- **10** 10mm jump rings
- **36** headpins
- 22 gauge wire

Note In right-angle weave, you may not be exiting the bead in the same orientation as described. If you are exiting opposite the side of the shared bead, use the illustration to understand which beads to pick up.

○	15º seed bead, color A
◔	11º seed bead, color B
●	8º seed bead, color A
◍	3mm pearl, color D
◆	4mm bicone crystal, color E
▲	4mm loch rosen, color F
⬡	12mm cosmic bead
⬭	14x10 oval bead

Row 1

Round 1

Pick up three color C 8º seed beads and an E 4mm bicone crystal. Repeat three times for a total of four groups. Tie a square knot **(figure 1)**.

Round 2

Pass through the first three Cs and the E. Pick up a C and pass through the next E. Repeat three times for a total of four Cs. Pass through the first C in round 2 **(figure 2)**.

Round 3

Pick up three color B 11º seed beads and pass through the next C from round 2. Repeat three times for a total of four groups. Pass through the first and second B in round 3 **(figure 3)**.

Round 4

Pick up a C, and pass through the middle B bead of the second group of Bs added in round 3. Repeat three times for a total of

four Cs. Weave to exit a shared side bead **(figure 4)**. Pick up a C, an E, three Cs, an E, and a C, and pass through the shared C from the first unit. Complete as in rounds 2–4.

Add units off of each shared bead to reach the length desired (11 units is 7½ in.).

Row 2

Weave to a side shared bead. Pick up a C, an E, three Cs, an E, three Cs, an E, three Cs, an E, and a C, and pass through the shared C from the opposite side to form a loop **(figure 5)**. Complete as in rounds 2–4. Weave to a top shared bead.

Pick up a C, an E, and a C, and pass through the shared side bead on the first strip of diamonds. Pick up a C, an E, three Cs, an E, three Cs, an E, and a C, and pass through the top shared bead on the first medallion **(figure 6)**. Complete as in rounds 2–4. Repeat for the same number of units as are in row 1.

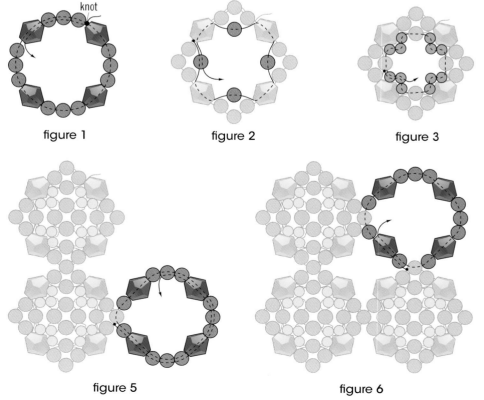

figure 1

figure 2

figure 3

figure 4

figure 5

figure 6

Toggle

Pick up 18 color A 15° seed beads and work in peyote stitch for a total of 20 rows or enough to fit around a cocktail straw. Zip the tube closed. With a 2-in. length of 22-gauge wire, turn a small loop at one end. Pick up an E and pass the wire through the toggle. Pick up an E and turn a second small loop to secure.

Anchor a double thread in the beads and exit the center of the toggle. Pick up a color F 4mm lochrosen and an A, and pass back through the F. Pierce the straw and exit the toggle directly opposite the F. Pick up an E and 13 Cs, and loop around the beads between two end diamonds. Pass back through the first C and the E. Weave off **(figure 7)**.

Embellishments

Using headpins, wirewrap the Swarovski beads of your choice. Pair pearls with lochrosen components. For pendants, attach a jump ring. Open a large jump ring around the intersection of two diamonds. String three or four dangles **(figure 7)** and close the jump ring. Repeat for each intersection with the exception of the last, which is left unembellished to incorporate the toggle bar.

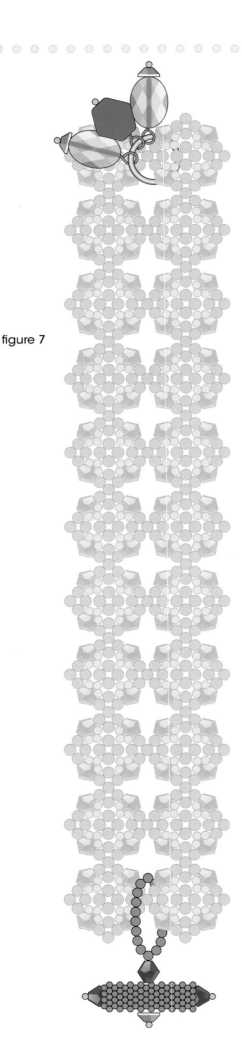

figure 7

MARCIA

Marcia DeCoster teaches national and international workshops specializing in beadweaving designs. Her work has been published in *The Art and Elegance of Beadweaving* by Carol Wilcox Wells, and she was one of the showcased artists in *Masters: Beadweaving*. Marcia was a 2009 Designer of the Year for *Beadwork* magazine and was recognized as one of the Bead&Button Show's Top Ten Teachers in 2010. Marcia is the author of *Marcia DeCoster's Beaded Opulence*. Marcia was named a Swarovski Ambassador in 2011.

maddesignsbeads.blogspot.com
create-your-style.com/Content.Node/
ambassadors/Marcia-DeCoster.php

"...to be asked to share the love of crystal, what could be better?"

How long have you been making jewelry?
I've been creating beadwoven jewelry since 1993. In 2004 I left my corporate career in information technology to be a full-time bead artist.

Best advice you've received?
Not every piece needs to be profound, given to me by my husband. He often will point out that a piece is complete when I might be tempted to bead more.

Favorite tool?
I love my Tulip awl for taking out intricate thread paths and for breaking beads out in the event that I've counted wrong. It is never far from reach. I also love my Gingher scissors, which are decorative and colorful.

Best thing about being an Ambassador?
The sparkle! Seriously though, I have always been a huge fan of SWAROVS-KI ELEMENTS, using many in my work, so to be asked to share the love of crystal, what could be better?

Favorite of the SWAROVSKI ELEMENTS?
Well, judging by my collection, I guess I'd have to say the 3mm Xilion bead, but I must say I can't think of one I don't like. The large pendants always captivate me, as do the beautiful fancy stones and large rivolis.

Inspiration?
Vintage jewelry, color, mood, and fashion all come into play in my work at various times.

Advice for new beaders?
It is always a good idea to take the time to learn the fundamentals. By building a good set of basic skills, you will have the ability to complete quality beadwork.

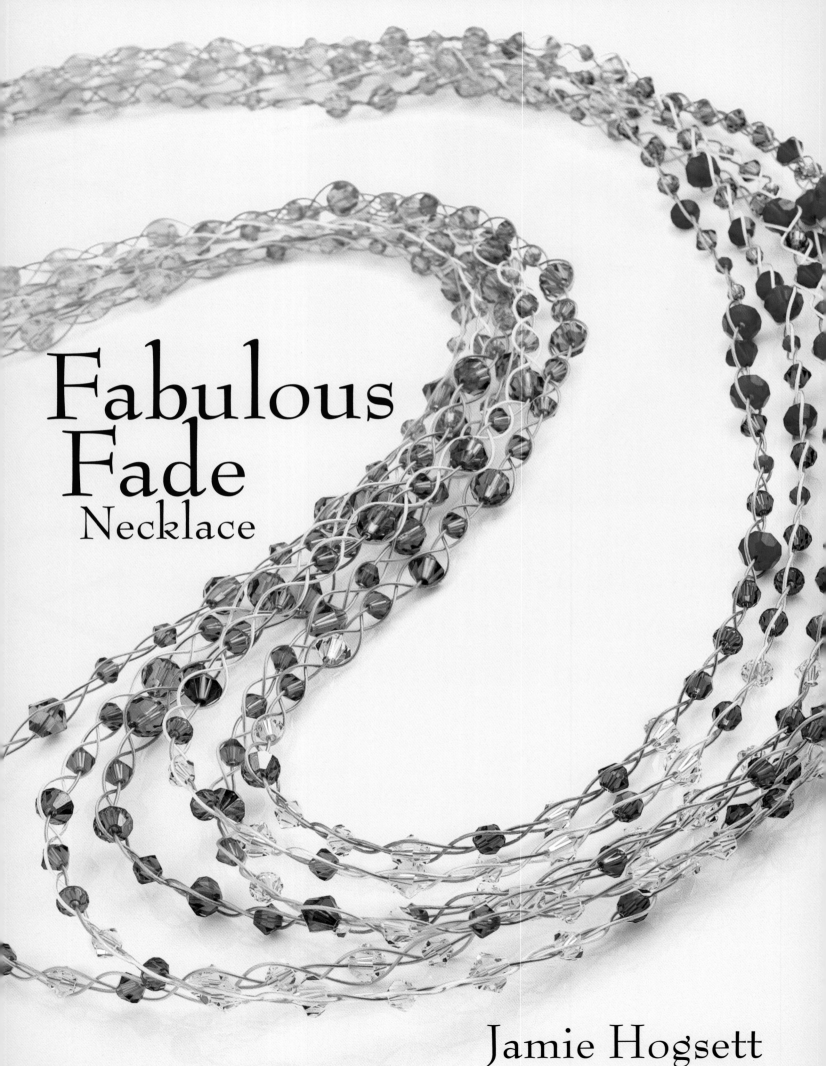

Fabulous
Fade
Necklace

Jamie Hogsett

When it comes to crystals, how do you choose which color to use? With this versatile project, you don't need to pick just one—we'll use 12! The length of this piece allows you to wear it in one generous strand, doubled as a choker, or even with a loose knot carefully tied into a focal point. The ombré effect of the colors fading seamlessly from one to another is amplified by the different colors of beading wire. Adding to the texture of the piece are a few different sizes of both bicone and round crystal shapes. Use this technique with any crystal colors to create a perfectly blended beauty.

materials

SWAROVSKI ELEMENTS
- 5328 Xilion beads
  - **9** 6mm Olivine
  - **8** 6mm Khaki
  - **15** 5mm Caribbean Blue Opal
  - **17** 5mm Light Azore
  - **18** 5mm Golden Shadow
  - **9** 4mm Violet Opal
  - **15** 4mm Violet
  - **15** 4mm Tanzanite
  - **17** 4mm Indicolite
  - **25** 4mm Light Azore

- **33** 4mm Olivine
- **19** 4mm Khaki
- **20** 4mm Lime
- **24** 4mm Jonquil
- 5000 rounds
  - **20** 6mm Violet
  - **14** 6mm Caribbean Blue Opal
  - **15** 6mm Khaki
  - **6** 6mm Lime
  - **10** 6mm Light Topaz
  - **28** 4mm Violet Opal
  - **7** 4mm Violet
  - **12** 4mm Tanzanite

- **25** 4mm Indicolite
- **5** 4mm Jonquil
- **19** 4mm Golden Shadow
- **15** 3mm Tanzanite
- **13** 3mm Caribbean Blue Opal
- **16** 3mm Lime
- **32** 3mm Light Topaz
- **13** 3mm Jonquil

Other supplies
- 24 2x2mm crimp tubes, silver
- 24 3mm crimp covers, silver
- 3-strand flower box clasp, silver
- beading wire (.019):
  - 480 in. Champagne
  - 192 in. 925 Sterling Silver
  - 192 in. 24K Gold

Tools
- crimping pliers
- wire cutters
- bead clamps

Stringing

1 Combine crystals of like colors into piles, one pile per color. You'll use crystal shapes and sizes randomly throughout; what's important is keeping track of the colors. Divide the Violet Opal and Crystal Golden Shadow crystals as follows: one pile of five crystals, three piles of six crystals, and two piles of seven crystals. Divide all other colors into six piles of six crystals each (**a**).

2 For Strand 1, use six-crystal piles of Violet Opal and Crystal Golden Shadow crystals. Place a bead clamp on one end of a 48-in. piece of Champagne wire. String four Violet Opals, a Violet, a Violet Opal, a Violet, a Violet Opal, three Violets, a Tanzanite, a Violet, a Tanzanite, a Violet, three Tanzanites, a Caribbean Blue Opal, a Tanzanite, a Caribbean Blue Opal, a

Tanzanite, three Caribbean Blue Opals, an Indicolite, a Caribbean Blue Opal, an Indicolite, a Caribbean Blue Opal, three Indicolites, a Light Azore, an Indicolite, a Light Azore, an Indicolite, three Light Azores, an Olivine, a Light Azore, an Olivine, a Light Azore, three Olivines, a Khaki, an Olivine, a Khaki, an Olivine, three Khakis, a Lime, a Khaki, a Lime, a Khaki, three Limes, a Light Topaz, a Lime, a Light Topaz, a Lime, three Light Topazes, a Jonquil, a Light Topaz, a Jonquil, a Light Topaz, three Jonquils, a Golden Shadow, a Jonquil, a Golden Shadow, a Jonquil, and four Golden Shadows (**b**). Place a bead clamp on the wire end and set aside.

3 Strand 2: repeat step 2.

4 Strand 3: Use seven-crystal piles of Violet Opal and Crystal Golden Shadow

a

crystals. Place a bead clamp on one end of a 48-in. piece of Champagne wire. String five Violet Opals, a Violet, a Violet Opal, a Violet, a Violet Opal, three Violets, a Tanzanite, a Violet, a Tanzanite, a Violet, three Tanzanites, a Caribbean Blue Opal, a Tanzanite, a Caribbean Blue Opal, a Tanzanite, three Caribbean Blue Opals, an Indicolite,

a Caribbean Blue Opal, an Indicolite, a Caribbean Blue Opal, three Indicolites, a Light Azore, an Indicolite, a Light Azore, an Indicolite, three Light Azores, an Olivine, a Light Azore, an Olivine, a Light Azore, three Olivines, a Khaki, an Olivine, a Khaki, an Olivine, three Khakis, a Lime, a Khaki, a Lime, a Khaki, three Limes, a Light Topaz, a Lime,

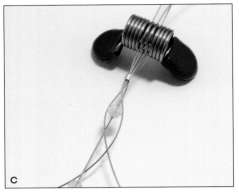

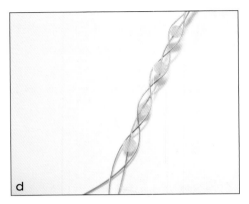

a Light Topaz, a Lime, three Light Topazes, a Jonquil, a Light Topaz, a Jonquil, a Light Topaz, three Jonquils, a Golden Shadow, a Jonquil, a Golden Shadow, a Jonquil, and five Golden Shadows. Place a bead clamp on the wire end and set aside.

5 Strand 4: Use seven-crystal piles of Violet Opal and Crystal Golden Shadow crystals. Place a bead clamp on one end of a 48-in. piece of Champagne wire. String six Violet Opals, a Violet, a Violet Opal, five Violets, a Tanzanite, a Violet, five Tanzanites, a Caribbean Blue Opal, a Tanzanite, five Caribbean Blue Opals, an Indicolite, a Caribbean Blue Opal, five Indicolites, a Light Azore, an Indicolite, five Light Azores, an Olivine, a Light Azore, five Olivines, a Khaki, an Olivine, five Khakis, a Lime, a Khaki, five Limes, a Light Topaz, a Lime, five Light Topazes, a Jonquil, a Light Topaz, five Jonquils, a Golden Shadow, a Jonquil, and six Golden Shadows. Place a bead clamp on the wire end and set aside.

6 Strand 5: Use the five-crystal piles of Violet Opal and Crystal Golden Shadow crystals. Place a bead clamp on one end of a 48-in. piece of Champagne wire. String four Violet Opals, a Violet, a Violet Opal, five Violets, a Tanzanite, a Violet, five Tanzanites, a Caribbean Blue Opal, a Tanzanite, five Caribbean Blue Opals, an Indicolite, a Caribbean Blue Opal, five Indicolites, a Light Azore, an Indicolite, five Light Azores, an Olivine, a Light Azore, five Olivines, a Khaki, an Olivine, five Khakis, a Lime, a Khaki, five Limes, a Light Topaz, a Lime, five Light Topazes, a Jonquil, a Light Topaz, five Jonquils,

a Golden Shadow, a Jonquil, and four Golden Shadows. Place a bead clamp on the wire end and set aside.

7 Strand 6: Use six-crystal piles of Violet Opal and Crystal Golden Shadow crystals. Place a bead clamp on one end of a 48-in. piece of Champagne wire. String five Violet Opals, a Violet, a Violet Opal, five Violets, a Tanzanite, a Violet, five Tanzanites, a Caribbean Blue Opal, a Tanzanite, five Caribbean Blue Opals, an Indicolite, a Caribbean Blue Opal, five Indicolites, a Light Azore, an Indicolite, five Light Azores, an Olivine, a Light Azore, five Olivines, a Khaki, an Olivine, five Khakis, a Lime, a Khaki, five Limes, a Light Topaz, a Lime, five Light Topazes, a Jonquil, a Light Topaz, five Jonquils, a Golden Shadow, a Jonquil, and five Golden Shadows. Place a bead clamp on the wire end and set aside.

Braiding

8 Secure two 48-in. pieces of Champagne beading wire in the first bead clamp of Strand 1, placing one wire on each side of the crystal strand and placing the bead clamp 2½ in. from the ends. Begin braiding the wires together. Every time the beaded wire passes to the middle of the braid, slide a crystal up into the braid **(c, d)**. Continue until all crystals are incorporated into the braid. Attach the end bead clamp to all three wires. Set aside.

9 Secure two 48-in. pieces of 925 Sterling Silver beading wire in the first bead stopper of Strand 2, placing one wire on each side of the crystal strand and placing the bead clamp 2½ in. from the wire ends. Repeat the process in step 8 to make a braided strand and set aside.

10 Secure two 48 in. pieces of 24K Gold beading wire in the first bead clamp of Strand 3, placing one wire on each side of the crystal strand and placing the bead clamp 2½ in. from the wire ends. Repeat the process in step 8 to make a braided strand and set aside.

11 Repeat step 8 for Strand 4, step 9 for Strand 5, and step 10 for Strand 6.

Crimping and Finishing

12 Line the strands up in order on your workspace. Make sure that each strand is slightly longer than the previous strand, removing beads from the ends of the braids, if necessary.

13 Carefully remove the first bead clamp from Strand 1. String a crimp tube over all three wire ends. Snug the crimp as close to the end of the braid as possible and crimp. Cut two wire ends. Cover the crimp with a crimp cover. Use the remaining wire end to string a crimp tube and the inside loop of one half of the clasp. Go back through the crimp, leaving a small loop of wire, and crimp. Cover the crimp with a crimp cover. Repeat on the other end of the strand, using the other clasp half.

14 Repeat step 13 using Strand 2, attaching the wires to the same loops of the clasp.

15 Repeat step 13 using Strand 3, attaching the wires to the middle loops of the clasp. Repeat using Strand 4.

16 Repeat step 13 using Strand 5, attaching the wires to the outside loops of the clasp. Repeat using Strand 6.

Jamie Hogsett is a bead lover, jewelry designer, and beading educator, currently creating for Antelope Beads. In previous bead-related journeys, she was education coordinator for Soft Flex Company and the editor of *Stringing* magazine. Jamie is the coauthor of *Show Your Colors!* and author of *Stringing Style* and the *Create Jewelry* series. She loves working with handmade beads and gemstones, and always adds a bit of crystal sparkle to her pieces. Although wireworking and stringing are her favorites, she adores seed bead work and can't wait for the day when she has time to sit and stitch. She enjoys life in Colorado, surrounded by family and the Rocky Mountains.

create-your-style.com/Content.Node/
ambassadors/Jamie-Hogsett.en.php

"I'm continually grateful that I get to make a living playing with beads."

How long have you been making jewelry?
Growing up the daughter of fine-jewelry store owners, I've been surrounded by jewelry my entire life. As long as I can remember, I've loved tinkering with the random tools and gemstones on my father's workbench. I've been making jewelry ever since, knotting friendship bracelets in elementary school and graduating to making beaded jewelry when I found my mom's stash of old macramé materials shoved into a closet. College brought an internship with a beading magazine and I was hooked. I'm continually grateful that I get to make a living playing with beads.

Best advice you've received?
I've been fortunate to learn from so many masters in this industry, it's difficult to pick just one bit. The piece of advice that I most often pass along to others came from Kate McKinnon, who recommended using crimping pliers to ensure the end of wire in a wrapped loop curves perfectly into the wrap. It's simple, but oh! such a great revelation.

Favorite tool?
Crimping pliers are wonderful. There are so many possibilities of what one can create with crimping pliers and crimp tubes.

Best thing about being an Ambassador?
Getting to know my fellow ambassadors—they're all so friendly, and they're passionate about SWAROVSKI ELEMENTS to boot!

Favorite of the SWAROVSKI ELEMENTS?
The Xilion bead (upgraded bicone). It's the first shape of crystal I ever used and is still my favorite. It looks lovely on its own, is great for helping to fill holes in large beads, works great in many different types of beading projects (stringing, wirework, knitting, stitching, etc. …), and is available in as many colors as I can imagine.

Inspiration?
What doesn't inspire me?! I'm inspired by books of all sorts, art, fonts, quotations, nature, animals, color, architecture, fashion, animation, even food. Family and friends are constant sources of inspiration, as are people I pass on the street who are wearing something that catches my eye.

Advice for new beaders?
Practice, practice, practice! Wrapped loops were once my nemesis. Only after making dozens and dozens of horrid attempts did I come away with anything to be proud of. Same with crimping—it often takes many tries to make a perfect crimp. You can do it though—don't give up!

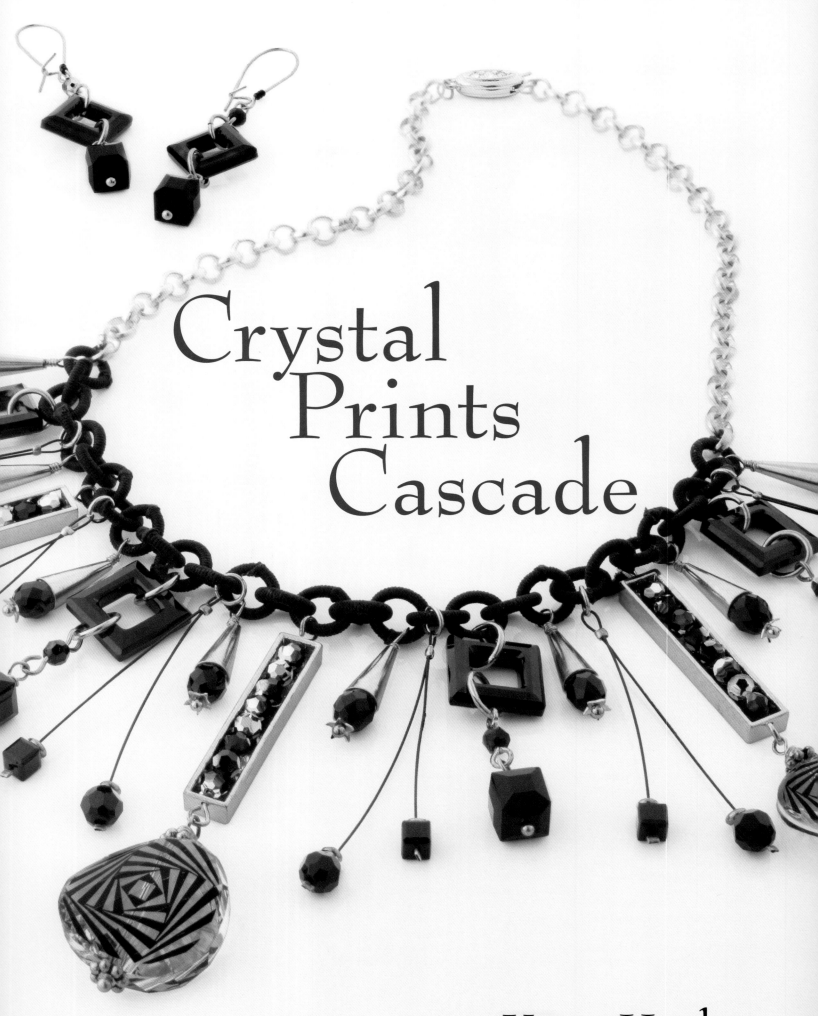

Crystal Prints Cascade

Katie Hacker

I love crystal prints! They're unusual and add a bit of dramatic flair to any design. I created this necklace with a little black dress in mind. You could wear a simpler necklace with your LBD and a cardigan during the day, and then slip this necklace on to amp up your style for the evening. Cascade necklaces work well with a variety of necklines, so it's a versatile look that can suit almost any style. Use the same pattern with different crystals for a completely different effect.

materials

SWAROVSKI ELEMENTS

- **4** 14mm 4439 square rings, Jet
- **8** 9x6mm 5500 teardrops, Jet
- 5000 round
    - **6** 6mm Jet
    - **28** 4mm Jet
- 5601 cube
    - **4** 8mm Jet
    - **6** 4mm Jet
- 5621 twist beads
    - 22mm Zebra Print
    - **2** 14mm Zebra Print

Other Supplies

- **3** rectangular Katiedids channel findings
- **12** 4mm solid rings, silver
- **6** 6mm rondelles, antique silver
- **8** bead cones, silver
- **8** ball-and-star headpins, silver
- **7** medium ball headpins, silver
- **7** eyepins, silver
- **8** 8mm jump rings, silver
- **10** 6mm jump rings, silver
- **2** 4mm jump rings, silver
- oval upper clasp, silver
- **18** #1 crimp beads, silver
- 29-link piece of polyester chain, black
- medium rolo chain, silver
- .018 Beadalon 19-strand beading wire, black

Tools

- roundnose pliers
- chainnose pliers
- wire cutters
- crimping pliers

1 On a ball headpin, string a 6mm spacer, a Zebra Print bead, and a spacer. Make a wrapped loop.

2 Connect an eyepin loop to the wrapped loop on the crystal prints dangle. String a rectangle component with eight 4mm rounds inside. Make a plain loop above the rectangle. Repeat Steps 1 and 2 for the remaining two Zebra Print beads.

3 Attach the large crystal prints dangle to the center link on the polyester chain. Skip seven links on each side of the pendant and attach the other crystal prints dangles (links 7 and 23) to begin the basic cascade pattern.

4 On a ball-and-star headpin, string a teardrop bead (point up) and a cone. Make a wrapped loop to attach it to the first link on the polyester chain. Repeat to attach teardrop/cone dangles evenly spaced across the polyester chain (links 1, 5, 9, 13, 17, 21, 25, 29).

5 On a ball headpin, string a cube and make a wrapped loop. Connect an eyepin loop to the wrapped loop, then string a 4mm jet round and make a plain loop. Use a 6mm jump ring to connect the loop to a jet square ring.

6 Repeat step 5 three more times, then attach the dangles on the polyester chain (evenly spaced at links 3, 11, 19, 27).

7 Cut six 4-in. pieces of beading wire. Fold each wire in half, string a crimp bead over both ends, and make a folded crimp ¼ in. below the fold.

8 String a silver solid ring, a 6mm round, and a crimp onto one end. Flatten the crimp to secure. Trim the other end slightly shorter and string a silver solid ring, a 4mm cube, and a crimp. Flatten the crimp. Repeat with the remaining wires.

9 Use a 6mm jump ring to connect a tasseled dangle to links 2, 8, 12, 17, 21, and 25.

10 Cut two pieces of rolo chain to bring the necklace to the desired length. Open the first link on each chain and connect it to one end of the polyester chain (or use additional jump rings).

11 Use a jump ring to attach half of the clasp to each end of the necklace.

Earrings

materials

SWAROVSKI ELEMENTS
- **2** 4mm 5000 rounds, Jet
- **2** 8mm 5601 cubes, Jet
- **2** 14mm 4439 square rings, Jet

Other Supplies
- **6** black oval Bead Bumpers
- **4** silver 8mm jump rings
- **2** silver eyepins
- **2** silver medium ball headpins
- **2** silver kidney-shaped earring wires

1 On an eyepin, string a 4mm round and make a plain loop above the bead. Attach the dangle to the earring wire.

2 Open an 8mm jump ring and connect the lower eyepin loop and a square crystal ring.

3 On a headpin, string a cube bead and make a wrapped loop above the bead.

4 Open an 8mm jump ring and connect the headpin loop and the crystal square ring.

5 Slide three Bead Bumpers onto the earring wire.

6 Make a second earring.

Katie Hacker is the host of the public television program, *Beads, Baubles & Jewels*. She has written many books about beading and jewelry making and is a columnist for *Bead Style* magazine. She is a Beadalon design team member and has her own line of jewelry findings, Katiedids Creative Components, available from Beadalon distributors.

KatieHacker.com.
create-your-style.com/Content.Node/
ambassadors/Katie-Hacker.en.php

"There's nothing like SWAROVSKI ELEMENTS for drama and sparkle."

How long have you been making jewelry?

I started making jewelry as a teenager because I couldn't find cool clip earrings for my unpierced ears. I wrote my first book, *It's Knot Hard: Hemp Jewelry,* right after college and have been building my career ever since. I feel really lucky to get to do what I love for a living.

Best advice you've received?

Be as patient with yourself as you are with others.

Favorite tool?

My Italian flush cutters are never far from my hands. The handles are comfortable and the cuts are clean.

Best thing about being an Ambassador?

My favorite part of being an Ambassador is the sense of camaraderie—we have a great time together!

Favorite of the SWAROVSKI ELEMENTS?

I'm partial to the crystal prints because they're so unusual. You just don't see them everywhere, so they're very eye-catching.

Inspiration?

I'm inspired by beautiful materials and there's nothing like SWAROVSKI ELEMENTS for drama and sparkle.

Advice for new beaders?

Everyone gets frustrated when their loops aren't perfect. Keep practicing! You will keep getting better and better.

Totally in Love

Monica Han

There are several heart-shaped SWAROVSKI ELEMENTS beads and pendants that totally capture my imagination. I used Wild Heart beads, Devoted 2 U, and Truly in Love Heart pendants to make this one-of-a-kind wirewrapped necklace. I chose Red Magma, Astral Pink, and Copper colors to express the feelings of warmth and love.

materials

SWAROVSKI ELEMENTS

- **2** 17x14mm 5743 Wild Heart bead, Red Magma
- 17x13mm 6261 Devoted 2 U pendant, Aastral Pink
- 18x15mm 6264 Truly in Love Heart pendant, Astral Pink

Other Supplies

- 16 in. 16-gauge round wire, copper
- 7½ ft. 24-gauge round wire, copper
- 18 in. 7mm heavy chain, copper
- 15mm toggle, copper

Tools

- chainnose pliers
- roundnose pliers
- wire cutters
- ruler

Please note: Directions are for a 20½-in. necklace with pendant.

1 Cut a 12-in. piece of 16-gauge wire. Bend in the middle to make a large heart shape while turning both sides into two smaller hearts, larger than the Wild Heart bead. Wrap once on each side to secure. Trim the ends (**a, left**). Cut a 4-in. piece of 16-gauge wire. Turn it into a small heart (**a, right**). This heart needs to be slightly larger than the Devoted 2 U pendant, and it needs to fit inside the piece on the left.

2 Cut five 3-in. pieces of 24-gauge wire. Wrap to connect the two pieces from step 1 in five spots as pictured (**b**).

3 Cut a 2-ft. piece of 24-gauge wire. Beginning at the top where the two small hearts meet, wrap over the upper right heart and string a Wild Heart bead. Go to the bottom diagonally and wrap the wire around the frame. Wrap over the wire below the bottom hole of the Wild Heart

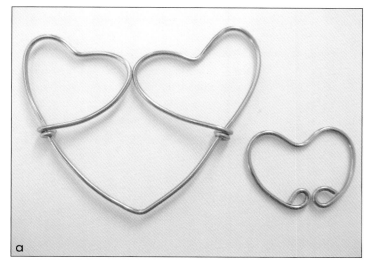

a

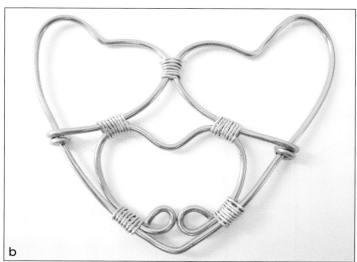

b

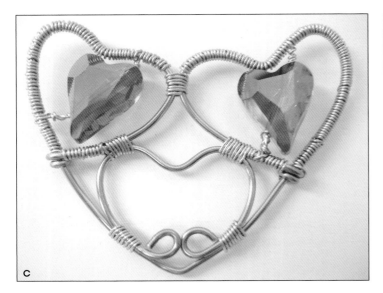

c

d

e

f

bead three or four times. Extend the wire behind the Wild Heart bead, and then wrap over the wire above the top hole of the Wild Heart bead to stabilize it. Continue to wrap the frame. Be careful in handling the wire to avoid kinks. Repeat on the left side (c).

4 Cut a 2-ft. piece of 24-gauge wire. Start wrapping the outline on the lower left. When you reach the center of the heart, string a Devoted 2 U pendant and make two wraps through the pendant. Continue to wrap the rest of the outline (d).

5 Cut a 3-in. piece of 24-gauge wire. Make a set of wraps through the Truly in Love pendant, and make a wrapped loop to connect it to the bottom of the large heart (e).

6 Cut two 9-in. pieces of chain. Open an end link and attach it to one side of the pendant. Repeat on the other side. Open the remaining end link and attach half a toggle clasp. Repeat on the other side (f).

MONICA

Monica Han started beading in 2002 and began teaching in 2005. She has received several awards from CREATE YOUR STYLE with SWAROVSKI ELEMENTS and Fire Mountain Gems design contests. Her projects have been published in *Bead Style*, *Step-by-Step Wire*, and *Belle Armoire* magazines. Monica became a CREATE YOUR STYLE Ambassador in 2009. Her specialties are wireworking and right-angle weave. She has taught at Bead Fest in Philadelphia, CREATE YOUR STYLE in Tucson, and her local bead stores.

cysdreambeads.blogspot.com
create-your-style.com/Content.Node/
ambassadors/Monica-Han.en.php

"Try different techniques, materials, and color combinations."

How long have you been making jewelry?
I have been beading since 2002. I was hooked when I got my first beading book.

Best advice you've received?
Have an open mind.

Favorite tool?
Since I love wireworking, I have to say chainnose pliers. I have one pair with small noses—they can reach small spaces and smooth wire ends.

Best thing about being an Ambassador?
Getting to know other talented Ambassadors and wonderful Swarovski staff. And of course being able to play with various SWAROVSKI ELEMENTS.

Favorite of the SWAROVSKI ELEMENTS?
Crystal Pearls, because there are many appealing colors, shapes, and sizes.

Inspiration?
People.

Advice for new beaders?
Try different techniques, different materials, and different color combinations.

Whitewashed Garden Bib

Renata Sánchez Ramos

This necklace represents the essence of the design aesthetic of Fou Fou Chat by the Terror Sisters, the business I run with my sister, Nadia. It's romantic and feminine like the brand, but at the same time is both classic and avant garde. The mixture of textures, techniques, and materials speaks to our signature look. The Crystal Pearls are the protagonists of my designs, and they mix with the delicate and elegant sparkle of the crystal and filigrees.

materials

SWAROVSKI ELEMENTS
- **3** strands 8mm 5850 Crystal Pearls, Powder Almond, Petrol
- **24** 9x8mm 5826 curved pearls, Crystal Bronze or Powder Almond
- **45** 4mm 5328 Xilion beads, Crystal Golden Shadow
- **8** 5030 8mm lucerna beads, Crystal Golden Shadow
- **25** 5mm 5000, Light Colorado Topaz AB
- 5742 10mm heart, Crystal Golden Shadow
- 19x11.5mm 4756 galactic flat fancy stone, Crystal Golden Shadow
- **16** 2028 flatback (no hot fix) SS12, Sand Opal
- **2** 6x4mm 4320 fancy stone, Vintage Rose
- 53203 SS29 chaton monté, Crystal
- **10** 57700 channels SS29TB0F131128, Crystal Golden Shadow
- 62000 filigree S2400F1A1028F, Crystal Golden Shadow, Black Diamond
- 62004 filigree S2400CF1S1028F, Smoked

Topaz, Light Smoked Topaz, Light Colorado Topaz
- 1028 Xilion chaton
  - ss29 Light Grey Opal
  - **22** pp21 Silver Shade
  - pp21 Vintage Rose
- 4228 Xilion navette
  - **2** 8x4mm Crystal Golden Shadow
  - **3** 8 4x2mm White Opal
- 4470 fancy stone
  - 12mm Crystal
  - 12mm Metal Setting H20
- 5810 Crystal Pearls, round
  - 10mm Crystal Vintage Gold
  - **5** 8mm Crystal Cream
  - **30** 6mm Crystal White
  - **28** 3mm Crystal White
  - **66** 4mm Crystal Bronze

Other Supplies
- 10g two-part epoxy clay, white (5g A/5g B part)
- ½ yd. elastic mesh, champagne or similar color

- 7 in. satin or silk ribbon, champagne or similar color
- lobster claw clasp, gold
- 54 in. flexible beading wire
- **2** 8mm jump rings, gold
- **2** 5mm jump rings, gold
- **10** 4mm jump rings, gold
- **10** 3mm jump rings, gold
- **20** crimp beads
- 28mm brass flower
- nylon thread

Tools
- vinyl or latex gloves
- flatnose pliers
- roundnose pliers
- silicon or resin flower mold
- tweezers
- beeswax-tipped toothpick
- yo-yo maker (I used Clover)
- scissors
- needle
- epoxy clay crystallized flower

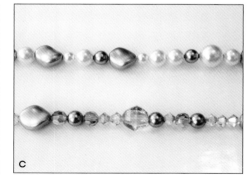

1 Wearing gloves, mix the two parts of epoxy clay. Knead both parts together for several minutes until clay is completely mixed and no longer looks marbled. (Working time is approximately 40 minutes to one hour after mixed.)

2 Form the clay into the mold and press it carefully. Wipe away the excess and remove the clay flower from the mold (**a**).

3 Place the galactic flat fancy stone and the rest of the bigger stones and chatons: Using a beeswax-tipped toothpick, pick up small round stones and other fancy stones and place them into clay. Follow the pattern as shown on the picture (**b**) or create your own.

4 Use the non-waxed side of the toothpick to make a hole on each side of the flower (to sew the flower to the fabric later). Set the pendant aside to cure (12–24 hours).

Necklace

5 Cut a 27-in. piece of beading wire. String assorted pearls and crystals as desired. I used: eight lucerna beads, 45 bicones, 25 round crystals, 27 small round pearls (bronze), and 8 curved pearls.

6 Cut a 27-in. piece of beading wire. String assorted pearls. I used: 15 curved pearls, 25 3mm white pearls, 23 4mm bronze pearls, 29 6mm white pearls and 5 8mm cream pearls (**c**).

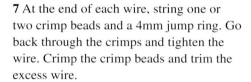

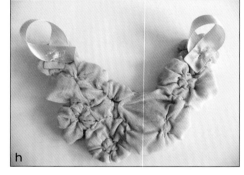

7 At the end of each wire, string one or two crimp beads and a 4mm jump ring. Go back through the crimps and tighten the wire. Crimp the crimp beads and trim the excess wire.

8 Repeat step 7 for the three strands of pre-strung pearls.

9 Connect one end of each strand from steps 7 and 8 with an 8mm jump ring (**d**). Braid the strands (**e**). At the end of the braid, connect the strands with an 8mm jump ring.

10 With 3mm jump rings, attach a five-channel length of 57700. Attach one end of the crystal channel chain to the 8mm jump ring at the end of the braid. Repeat on the other end.

11 At one end of the crystal channel chain, attach a lobster claw clasp with a 5mm jump ring. Attach a 5mm jump ring to the other end of the crystal channel chain.

Bib

12 With the help of the yo-yo maker, make three large and five medium yo-yos. For this project I used stretch mesh, but silk and cotton fabric also work well (**f**).

13 Insert the fancy stone 4470 into its setting and sew to the center of a small yo-yo with nylon thread (.2mm). Stitch 12 bronze pearls around it.

14 Place the filigree 62000 on a small yo-yo and stitch it with nylon thread. Repeat with the 62004 and a large yo-yo.

15 Stitch the heart bead to the center of a medium yo-yo. Stitch a curved pearl, a bronze pearl, and two small white pearls.

16 Stitch a bronze pearl, a white small pearl, a medium white pearl, and the chaton monté to a small yo-yo.

17 Stitch the brass flower to a large yo-yo. Stitch a 10mm pearl to the center.

18 Stitch the epoxy clay flower in the center of a large yo-yo, using two bronze pearls to hide the holes of the clay flower (**g**).

19 Join all the fabric flowers from the back using nylon thread and small stitches. On each side of the bib, stitch 3 in. of ribbon in order to fix it to the pearl and crystal braid (**h**).

Done! Your beautiful Whitewashed Crystal Garden Bib Necklace is finished. If you wish, you can wear it as a statement necklace or remove the fabric piece for a more classical look. It's a two-in-one lovely piece, isn't it?

RENATA

Photo: David Dahlhaus 2011

Renata Sánchez Ramos works and lives in Mexico City. In addition to her BA in clinical psychology, she has studied art therapy and has taken workshops in silversmithing, lost wax, handbag construction, shoe design, haute couture millinery, recycled paper, and more. She has taught jewelry workshops in Mexico and the United States. Renata coordinated the Gray Area Gris, an International Contemporary Jewelry Symposium (Mexico City, 2010). In 2008, she and her sister Nadia founded Fou Fou Chat by the Terror Sisters, a fashion accessories brand. Their pieces have been published in magazines including *Harper's Bazar, Elle, Vogue, InStyle,* and *Nylon* (Mexican editions).

foufouchat.com
create-your-style.com/Content.Node/
ambassadors/Renata-Sanchez-Ramos.php

"Is it comfortable? Is it wearable? Does it make you feel good?"

How long have you been making jewelry?
I started as a hobby when I was 17, and it remained one of my favorite activities. However, it wasn't until 2008 that I decided to make it professionally: it became my main interest and passion.

Best advice you've received?
You always have to think if you would be able to use and wear that piece that you have just made. Is it comfortable? Is it wearable? Does it make you feel good? If your answer is no for any of these questions, then you have to go back and do something about it.

Favorite tool?
The basic tools are always the best: flat and roundnose pliers, the crochet hook … even if you have no tools at all, it's your creativity which will lead you to create something extraordinary.

Best thing about being an Ambassador?
Now I know what it means to be a CREATE YOUR STYLE with SWAROVSKI ELEMENTS Ambassador. You have the privilege to see the trends and innovations before they are launched. Also, it's a pleasure to share my work and passion for SWAROVSKI ELEMENTS, design, and DIY techniques with all ambassadors and customers.

Favorite of the SWAROVSKI ELEMENTS?
I'm in love with Crystal Pearls: round, baroque, and pear shapes. Recently, the Wave family has amazed me. Wave beads and pendants are absolutely gorgeous.

Inspiration?
It's quite easy to find inspiration in the materials by themselves … but also, I get inspired by movies, nature, fashion, music, and architecture.

Advice for new beaders?
Don't limit yourself to certain techniques and materials. Try new possibilities and applications. Find your own voice and let it be your guide when designing.

Rainforest
Necklace

Nadia Sánchez Ramos

This project was totally inspired by the SWAROVSKI ELEMENTS Earth trend. I'm celebrating wildlife in the rainforest. Close your eyes and feel the luscious leaves tickling your neck, and relish in the joy of wearing a little dragonfly: When you wear it, you will also think of nature's beauty and perfection. I chose an assortment of beads, sew-on stones, pendants, fancy stones, and buttons—you can easily switch colors, products, and sizes to fit your personal taste. This necklace uses no chain, clasps, or jump rings—only glue, monofilament, SWAROVSKI ELEMENTS, and crimps in a slightly different way. The piece looks good on both sides, too, due to careful finishing. There are many ideas and possibilities in this necklace to use in your own projects!

materials

SWAROVSKI ELEMENTS

- **12** 12mm 3015 rivoli button, Chrysolite
- **2** 12mm 3017 square button, Padparadscha
- **2** 19x11.5mm 3256 sew-on rhinestones, Crystal Golden Shadow
- 10mm 3200 two-hole sew-on rivoli, Crystal Bronze Shadow
- 8mm 3700 margarita, Crystal Volcano or Crystal Vitrail Medium.
- **12** 10mm 5000B ceramic faceted round, Marbled Terracotta
- **4** 6mm 5754 butterfly, Crystal Copper or Crystal Bronze Shade
- **5** 9x6mm 5500 teardrop, Peridot or Peridot AB
- **4** 23mm 6690 wing pendants, Crystal or Light Colorado Topaz
- **2** 14mm 4737 triangle ring, Crystal Copper

- 14mm 4139 cosmic ring, Crystal Copper
- 12 or 14mm 5810 pearl, Brown
- 8mm 47508 silver round ball, Erinite
- **2** 8mm 5000 faceted rounds, Copper
- 30cm 59000 or 59100 yarn, Brown and pearls or Green and crystal
- 3128 sew-on lochrosen
    8–10 5mm Fern Green or Palace Green Opal
    12 3mm Light Grey Opal
    5 5mm Mocha
    8–10 3mm Mocha
    3 5mm Crystal Copper
- 5203 polygon
    4 18x12mm Light Colorado Topaz
    18x12mm Padparadscha
- 5301 bicone
    44 4mm Smoked Topaz
    60 4mm Crystal Copper
    40 2.5mm Mocha

- 5040 rondelle
    8mm Fern Green
    6 6mm Topaz blend

Other Supplies

- 1 gram seed beads
- ⅛ yd. pleather
- monofilament (.9-1mm)
- nylon thread (.2mm) tin or copper
- flexible beading wire (.024)
- 3–4 crimps
- beading needle
- lighter or torch
- G-S Hypo Cement or E-6000 adhesive
- double-sided tape

Tools

- flatnose pliers
- roundnose pliers
- side cutters
- scissors
- toothpick or craft stick

Prepare the Leaves

1 Enlarge and copy the patterns (p. 112) on tracing paper. Mark front F and reverse R. With double-sided tape, stick the R side of each pattern to the pleather's textile side. Cut one piece each. Stick the F side to the reverse side of the pleather and cut one piece each. You'll have a pair for each leaf shape. Make one large round set, one small round set, and three eye-shaped sets.

2 Leaf A: On one piece of an eye-shaped leaf pair, sew eight 5mm 3128 Palace Green Opals in a straight line.

3 Glue the remaining pleather piece to the back of the first with reverse sides together; let dry. Punch holes at each end, 7–8mm from the points.

4 Leaf B: On one piece of a small round leaf pair, sew: two 3256 rhinestones, a 3200 rivoli, and four 5203 Light Colorado Topaz polygons. Sew 4mm 5301 Smoked Topaz bicones to cover visible gaps; fill in between the stones with 3mm 3128 Light Grey Opal lochrosens. Repeat step 3, punching the holes 4–5mm from the edges.

5 Leaf C: Spread a thin coat of glue on the back of each half of an eye-shaped leaf pair and glue together to make a double-sided leaf. Let dry. Fold the leaf vertically and use scissors to cut from ¾ in. inside the point, following the curve of the leaf shape and stopping near the top. Unfold. Punch a hole 4–5mm from each upper edge. Fold the tip down and punch a hole through both layers even with the side holes.

6 Leaf D: Knot a strand of Crystal or Pearl Yarn and burn the tip. Melt and press the tip on the back of the large round leaf. Bring the yarn to the front. Stitch with nylon thread to secure the yarn. Stretch the yarn to the opposite edge. Set by cutting and

melting the tip and pressing it on the back (leave at least ½ in. for this). Make a stitch to set the pearls. Repeat to form all surface lines. Sew five 5mm and eight 3mm mocha lochrosens, placing them all over the surface. Repeat step 3, punching the holes 4–5mm from the edges.

7 Leaf E: Spread a thin coat of glue on the backs of the remaining eye-shaped leaf pair and glue together to make a double-sided leaf. Let dry. Punch holes in the center,

a

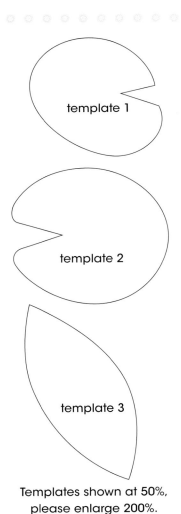

template 1

template 2

template 3

Templates shown at 50%,
please enlarge 200%.

b

c

22mm from each point, and 7–8mm from each point for a total of five holes.

Dragonfly

8 Legs: Cut an 8-in. piece of 28-gauge wire. String a 2.5mm Mocha bicone. Wrap the wire end around the bead. String four 2.5mm Mocha bicones. Make a loop with roundnose pliers, and string five 2.5mm Mocha bicones for the opposite leg, wrapping the wire end around the last bead. Make two more pairs of legs using seven 2.5mm Mocha bicones on each side.

9 Body: Center a 4mm Crystal Copper bicone on a 4-in. piece of 28-gauge wire. Twist once and string three Peridot AB teardrops over both wire ends. Separate the strands and string a Peridot AB teardrop on each end. Twist and string the longer pairs of legs. String an 8mm rondelle, the smaller pair of legs, and a 8mm round ball **(a)**. Wrap the wire around the ball three or four times. Use nylon thread to set the wing

pendants over the body **(b)** and finish with an 8mm margarita. Sew the dragonfly to the leaf through the center and adjacent holes.

Stringing

10 Cut a 9½-in. piece of monofilament. Burn the tip and form a ball. String: a butterfly, five 4mm Smoked Topaz bicones, a seed bead, and a crimp. Go through the hole of a square button (from foiled side to crystal side). String a butterfly and go back through the button hole and the crimp. Flatten the crimp. String 18 4mm Smoked Topaz bicones; a 6mm rondelle, six ceramic rounds, a 6mm rondelle, a Padparadscha polygon, a 6mm rondelle; a 12 or 14mm pearl, a 6mm rondelle, three or four seed beads, and a crimp. Sew through the first hole of Leaf A, string a square button, a butterfly, and go back through the second button hole exiting through the leaf hole and going back through the crimp. Flatten the crimp. Trim the excess monofilament, and burn the tip to form a ball.

Connect the Necklace

11 A to B: Cut a 5-in. piece of monofilament and burn the tip to form a ball. String a 3mm Light Grey Opal lochrosen, Leaf B through the first hole (from the back), and the second hole of Leaf A (exit front). String a 5mm Crystal Copper lochrosen, 19 4mm Crystal Copper bicones, a 14mm triangle, an 8mm Crystal Copper faceted round, and a 4mm Crystal Copper bicone. Trim the monofilament, and burn the tip to form a ball.

12 B to C to D: Cut a 3½-in. piece of monofilament and burn the tip to form a ball. String a 3mm Light Grey Opal lochrosen and the second hole of Leaf B (back to front). String three 12mm Chrysolite rivoli buttons (face front, face

back, and face front) **(c)**. Go through the first hole of leaf C from front to back. Sew back up through the center hole (top tip previously folded and pierced). String two 12mm rivoli buttons facing front, one facing back and one facing front. Sew through D from front to back. String a 3mm Light Grey Opal lochrosen. Trim the monofilament leaving a ½-in. tail. Hold thread with tweezers near the base and burn the tip to form a ball.

13 D to E: Cut a 17-in. piece of monofilament and burn the tip to form a ball. String a 4mm bicone, a 8mm faceted round, a 14mm cosmic triangle, 23 4mm Crystal Copper bicones, and a 5mm Crystal Copper lochrosen. Sew through the remaining hole in Leaf D and the first hole in Leaf E from front to back. String a 3mm Light Grey Opal lochrosen, nine seed beads, a 3mm Light Grey Opal lochrosen (the second hole from back to front), a 4mm Crystal Copper bicone, and go back through the same hole. String seed beads behind the leaf to the third hole. String a 5mm Copper lochrosen and go through from back to front.

14 String five or six 4mm Crystal Copper bicones, and a 14mm cosmic ring. Wrap the beads and the tip of leaf around the ring, and go through the hole. Come back through the fourth hole from back to front, string four 4mm crystal copper bicones, go under the first loop, and string four 4mm Crystal Copper bicones, five 12mm Chrysolite rivoli buttons in alternating facing front and back, a 4mm Crystal Copper bicone, a 6mm topaz blend rondelle, six ceramic faceted rounds, a 6mm rondelle, 14 4mm smoked topaz bicones, a crimp and 20 or 21 seed beads. Go back through the crimp and flatten it. String three 4mm Smoked Topaz bicones and a 6mm butterfly. Cut the thread, leaving a ½-in. tail. Burn the tip to form a ball.

Photo: David Dahlhaus 2011

Nadia Sánchez Ramos works and lives in Mexico City. Her BA degree is in fine arts with a specialty in cultural management. She learned basic silversmithing with Gabriel Ruiz Oteo and at the Research Center of Industrial Design of the Universidad Nacional Autónoma de México (CIDI-UNAM). Additional workshops include fashion accessories design, polymer, resin, washi zoquei, and haute couture millinery. Nadia coordinated the Gray Area Gris Contemporary Jewelry Symposium and Show (Mexico, 2010). Designing for Fou Fou Chat By The Terror Sisters since 2008, her work appears in magazines such as *Harper's Bazaar, Elle, InStyle, Vogue Blink,* and *Gatopardo.* Nadia has taught jewelry-making workshops in Mexico and the USA.

foufouchat.com
foufouchatbytheterrorsisters.blogspot.com
create-your-style.com/Content.Node/
ambassadors/Nadia-Sanchez-Ramos.php

"Always have a plan, but learn to be flexible and creative."

How long have you been making jewelry?
This has been a passion for me since I was 4 or 5 years old. I loved to spy in my mother's and aunt's jewelry boxes. I remember trying to make a queen's crown and a magic wand with aluminium foil. Later, at age 12, I was impressed by the jewels Frida Kahlo used in her pictures, and with Salvador Dali's surrealistic jewels (encyclopedias and art books were more interesting to me than TV, then). This led me to start collecting beautiful Indian and Mexican silver pieces or vintage bijoux. At age 18, I attended private courses with a wonderful silversmith and fine artist, Gabriel Ruiz Oteo, who introduced me to basic jewelry techniques. I made my own jewelry for years, until I realized this could become my main activity.

Best advice you've received?
To be very aware of the interaction between body gestures, tools, and materials.

Favorite tool?
A tool as simple as a needle, which you can find in every home on earth, can help you to construct, modify, embellish, or repair many things with particular love and care.

Best thing about being an Ambassador?
To have the opportunity to share what I've learned with fantastic teachers or use it on my own in the workshop. And of course, to share with creative and enthusiastic people my passion for SWAROVSKI ELEMENTS.

Favorite of the SWAROVSKI ELEMENTS?
Sew-on stones, the ceramics family, Crystal Pearls, baroque pendants, cupchains... I can't choose just one!

Inspiration?
Literature, art, movies, science, nature, and life.

Advice for new beaders?
Be patient: start with easy and simple projects, and increase difficulty gradually. Always have a plan, but learn to be flexible and creative.

Netted Twins
Necklace

Anna Elizabeth Draeger

The building blocks for my designs are SWAROVSKI ELEMENTS and seed beads. The challenge of pairing the right amount of crystals with the proper seed beads to create beautiful and wearable designs is the driving force every time I sit down to create with my beads, and this necklace with crystals, Crystal Pearls, crystal lentil beads, twin beads, and seed beads is no different. Weaving these elements together using a chevron technique and mostly crystals and pearls produced a fluid drape in the center portion, and switching to mainly seed beads created sturdy neck straps that can be adjusted for a perfect fit.

materials

SWAROVSKI ELEMENTS

- **15** 6mm 6200 pendants, Greige
- **42** 4mm 5328 bicones, White Opal
- **90** 3mm 5810 pearls, Crystal Deep Brown Pearl
- **44** 2mm 5000 rounds, Greige

Other supplies

- **112** (approximately) Twin beads, Czech brown iris
- 3–4g 15º seed beads, brown iris
- Fireline
- beading needles

1 Attach a stop bead to the center of 3 yd. (2.7m) of conditioned Fireline. Pick up a Twin bead, a 2mm round crystal, a Twin, a 15º seed bead, a 3mm pearl, a 15º, a 4mm bicone crystal, a 15º, a 3mm, a 15º, a Twin, a 2mm, a Twin, a 15º, a 3mm, a 15º, a 4mm, a 15º, a 3mm, a 15º, a Twin, a 2mm, a Twin, a 15º, a 3mm, a 15º, a 4mm, a 15º, three 6mm pendants, a 15º, a 4mm, a 15º, a 3mm, and a 15º **(figure 1, a–b)**. Sew back through the remaining hole of the last Twin picked up **(b–c)**.

2 Pick up a 2mm, and sew through the remaining hole of the next Twin **(c–d)**. Pick up a 15º, a 3mm, a 15º, a 4mm, a 15º, a 3mm, a 15º, a Twin, a 2mm, a Twin, a 15º, a 3mm, a 15º, a 4mm, a 15º, a 15º, a 3mm, and a 15º, and sew through the remaining hole of the next Twin **(d–e)**. Pick up a 2mm, and sew through the remaining hole of the next Twin **(e–f)**.

3 Pick up a 15º, a 3mm, a 15º, a 4mm, a 15º, a 3mm, a 15º, a Twin, a 2mm, a Twin, a 15º, a 3mm, a 15º, a 4mm, a 15º,

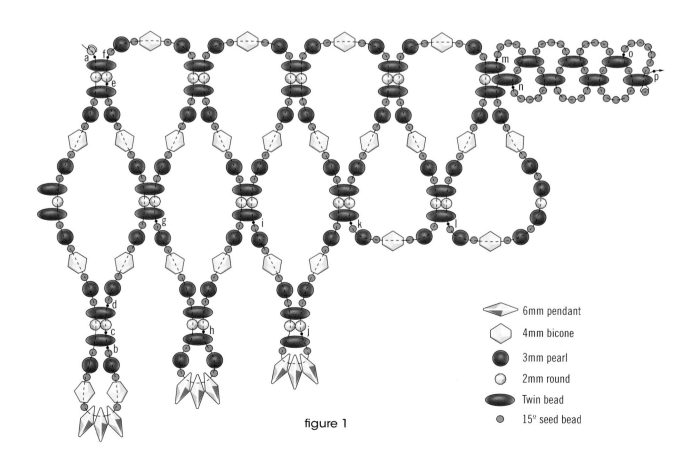

figure 1

6mm pendant

4mm bicone

3mm pearl

2mm round

Twin bead

15º seed bead

a 3mm, and a 15º, and sew back through the remaining hole of the next Twin from the previous step. Pick up a 2mm, and sew through the remaining hole of the next Twin (**f–g**).

4 Pick up a 15º, a 3mm, a 15º, a 4mm, a 15º, a 3mm, a 15º, a Twin, a 2mm, a Twin, a 15º, a 3mm, a 15º, three 6mms, a 15º, a 3mm, and a 15º, and sew back through the remaining hole of the last Twin picked up in this step (**g–h**).

5 Repeat steps 2 and 3 (**h–i**).

6 Pick up a 15º, a 3mm, a 15º, a 4mm, a 15º, a 3mm, a 15º, a Twin, a 2mm, a Twin, a 15º, three 6mms, and a 15º, and sew back through the remaining hole of the last Twin picked up in this step (**i–j**).

7 Repeat steps 2 and 3 (**j–k**).

8 Repeat step 3 twice (**k–l**).

9 Pick up a 15º, a 3mm, a 15º, a 4mm, a 15º, a 3mm, a 15º, a 3mm, a 2mm, a 3mm, a 15º, a 3mm, a 15º, a 4mm, a 15º, a 3mm, and a 15º. Sew back through the remaining hole of the last Twin picked up in the previous step, pick up a Twin, and sew through the remaining hole of the next Twin (**l–m**).

10 Pick up five 15ºs, a Twin, and a 15º, and sew back through the remaining hole of the Twin picked up in the previous step (**m–n**). Repeat this stitch 33 times, or until you reach half the desired length (**n–o**).

11 Pick up seven 15ºs, and sew through the remaining hole of the last Twin picked up. Pick up a 15º, and sew back through the same hole of the last Twin (**o–p**). End this thread.

12 Remove the stop bead from the remaining thread, and work steps 3–11 to complete the other half of the necklace.

Anna Elizabeth Draeger is a well-known jewelry designer and author of the books *Crystal Brilliance* and *Great Designs for Shaped Beads*. Some of the designs included in her shaped beads book are available as a three-part series of digital downloads, with each part featuring five designs using tiles and Tila beads, peanut beads, and drops. Her newest endeavor is a video class through CraftArtEdu.

originaldesignsbyanna.squarespace.com
create-your-style.com/Content.Node/
ambassadors/Anna-Draeger.en.php.

"If I had it my way, I'd bead all day, everyday."

How long have you been making jewelry?

I started using colorful seed beads and working on a loom in the early 1990s. There were not many bead stores then, so I spent a lot of time picking through low-quality beads to make Native American-inspired jewelry and patterns. I never expected beading to be my livelihood, but I taught classes at a store where the founding editor of *Bead&Button* shopped. She saw some of my class samples and asked if I'd like them to appear in the magazine. This was the start of my career as a designer for publication. I have been teaching since 1998, and it is still my favorite part of my life that pertains to jewelry.

Best advice you've received?

As a self-taught bead artist, I haven't received much in the way of advice, but I have received an unending supply of support and encouragement from my family, friends, and students. It is what keeps me going. I guess the best advice is to just keep on designing.

Favorite tool?

It is hard to choose a favorite tool because I LOVE tools. From the containers that hold my precious beads and crystals to the very basic needles and thread, I'd have to say I couldn't do what I do without them. My favorite tools are my hands, head, and heart, because my hands allow me to create the designs that my head thinks up, and my heart is filled with joy when I share what I do with others.

Best thing about being an Ambassador?

Being part of this group is like being a part of an extended family. Everyone loves what they do, and is open and happy to share, listen, encourage, and inspire. It is a community that strengthens my desire to be in this line of work.

Favorite of the SWAROVSKI ELEMENTS?

My absolute favorite element is the Xilion bead (upgraded bicone). I prefer 4mm and smaller. They are

the staple of most of my designs. The precise shape makes it easy to create geometric designs, and they work well with seed beads. I like all of the crystal, pearl, and fancy stone elements, and I would like to branch out a bit more to use other elements.

Inspiration?

Many things inspire me: colors, shapes, architecture but what often inspires me are the elements and beads. I'll see something and my mind immediately starts forming an idea, and then I start considering what beads, shapes, and techniques will work best with it. If I had it my way, I'd bead all day, everyday.

Advice for new beaders?

Find something that really appeals to you so if you get stuck along the way, you'll be motivated to keep trying. Take classes, read books, and find other beaders to help you. Use the tremendous community of creative people to inspire you!

Encaustic Pins

Debbi Simon

Encaustic is from the Greek word for " to burn in." It is a wonderful art medium that has been in use for ages. In ancient Greece, this incredibly durable material was used to adorn sculptures, murals, boats, and architecture. Encaustic saw a resurgence in the 1960s with artists such as Jasper Jones, but lost its momentum until recently. One reason I fell in love with encaustic is that the wax becomes hard and can be shined to an enamel-like finish. Over time, the oils from your hands will actually enhance the wax and offer patina-like qualities to the finished piece. It is the tactile, enamel-like property I wanted to showcase with crystals.

materials

SWAROVSKI ELEMENTS

- 1028 Xilion chatons in a variety of sizes and colors: pp12–pp25, Indicolite; pp18–pp24, Crystal Bronze Shade; pp18–pp21, Sand Opal
- fancy stones in a variety of shapes, sizes, and colors: 4428 square, Indicolite; 3.5x9.5mm 4200/2 navette; 12x4mm 2555 cosmic baguette, Silver Shade

Other supplies

- encaustic wax
- two-part mold material
- non-hardening clay, such as polymer
- found objects: vintage rhinestone jewelry
- Badger Balm
- two-part epoxy glue
- pin back
- screws
- eyepins
- an assortment of chain and vintage findings and charms
- Gilders paste or any acrylic or oil paints: German silver, copper, patina, iris blue
- isopropyl alcohol or GooGone

Tools

- tweezers
- toothpicks
- clear measuring cup
- craft knife
- heat gun or hair dryer
- Ranger Melt Art melting pot
- soft cotton cloth

Plan the Design and Make the Mold

1 Develop a design using vintage rhinestone jewelry, crystals, or found objects. Seek different textures or something a little unexpected. If jewelry is missing rhinestones, it is even better (see step 28). Start with small designs that are relatively flat. Simpler can be better.

2 Knead and roll out polymer clay about ½-in. thick.

3 With extra clay, fill any indentations on the backs of the jewelry or found objects.

4 Press the jewelry or found object into the clay. Push it down gently, and make sure the clay comes up around the piece and doesn't leave any holes or gaps.

5 Take any secondary design elements (smaller vintage pieces, charms, or crystals) and put a small, thin piece of extra clay on the back of each to eliminate gaps. Arrange and press gently into the design started in step 4 (**a**).

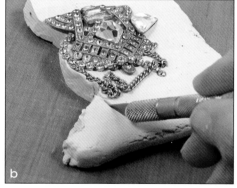

6 With a craft knife, clean up excess clay around the smaller pieces placed on top of the main piece.

7 With a craft knife, cut around the design to remove all excess clay. Cut closely around the piece to create the final shape (**b**).

8 Smooth the cut edges for a better mold.

9 Place the piece on a flat nonstick surface or a small plastic container with a flat bottom.

10 Following the manufacturer's directions for the molding material, mix equal parts of part A and part B (1:1 ratio). Be as precise as possible in your measurements (**c**). You only need to mix enough to coat your piece with a layer of mold material.

11 Slowly fold the two parts together with a stir stick. Scrape the sides and bottom of the measuring cup and stick as you are mixing to equally distribute both parts, and stir until the mixture is a solid color (**c**). Working time is usually up to 10 minutes after the material is mixed, but it can vary.

c

d

e

f

12 Slowly pour or drip the mold material over your piece, trying to cover it thoroughly. The mold material will self level, leaving a thin coat. As the material cures, it will expand, making the mold tighter and more accurate. Cure for about three hours.

13 Repeat steps 10–12, adding two or three additional layers of mold material to your piece (**d**). Wait about three hours between layers. The detail and stability you gain is worth the extra time and commitment. Your mold will be thicker and more durable. After the final layer, cure completely for three hours.

14 Remove the object from the mold. Be careful—the mold material is thin like a glove. It's durable, but you still want to be careful not to rip it.

15 Clean up the mold, removing any residue or little pieces of clay left behind.

tip There are a variety of mold materials available on the market. I recommend Rebound 25 by Smooth On. Look for YouTube videos with molding tips and techniques.

Make a Wax Casting

16 Remove the accent crystals from the original armature and clean off any clay or residue. Place the crystals like puzzle pieces into their respective spots in the mold (**e**). They will become part of the finished casting. Coat the crystal and the inside of the mold with a little Badger Balm. This is optional, but results in a tighter seal.

17 Turn the melting pot on and set the temperature to around 175–200° F. Add the wax to the melting pot. If the wax starts to smoke and smell, lower the

temperature. Add other colors if you want to customize your color. Completely melt the wax.

18 Carefully pour the melted wax into the mold (**f**) until the mold is half filled. Be careful; it's hot! Lift the mold and gently agitate, moving the hot wax around so it gets into every detail of the mold. Pour wax into the mold until it is almost full.

19 Leave the mold undisturbed while the wax cools. Before you take the casting out of the mold, put it in the freezer for 10–15 minutes so the wax will get a little bit harder and it will be easier to separate the casting from the mold.

20 Carefully remove the casting. Be careful not to pull off any pieces that might be sticking. If you take your time and work with it, nothing should break.

21 Using a craft knife, trim any excess wax from the casting. Pay special attention to the back where the edges are raised and should be cut back. Carve off anything that needs cleaning up or needs to be revised on the casting. (That's the beauty of working with wax—you can keep reworking the piece.)

22 Use a heat gun to heat and smooth the back of the piece. To clean up knife lines, use just enough heat for the top layer to become glossy. Pull the heat source away. You should have a nice flat finish.

23 Clean any residue from the crystals with isopropyl alcohol or Goo Gone.

24 With a soft cotton cloth, gently rub the wax. It will start to shine and take on an enamel-like quality.

25 Using a dark or Patina Gilders paste, rub color into the detail of the casting. Quickly remove the paste from the raised areas, leaving the color behind in the detail. Buff to return the shine of the wax.

26 Apply color to the raised areas with a lighter color gilders paste to help finish the design and add accents that highlight the great details of the casting.

27 Mix two-part epoxy following manufactures directions.

28 Apply a dab of glue where you want to place crystals. The natural bezels created from missing stones on the original piece are a good spot for new crystals. Fill the cavity half full with glue using a tool with a small pointed tip like a toothpick or needle tool. Let the glue sit for a few minutes to get tacky.

29 Pick up and apply the crystals with tweezers or a wax stick.

30 Apply mixed glue to the back of the brooch for the pin back. Gently hold the pin back in place until the glue begins to set a little. Put aside and allow the glue to cure completely.

Add Accent Chain

31 Open the eye of an eyepin. Attach different lengths of chain and close the eyepin. Repeat with a second eyepin at the other ends of the chain.

32 Poke a small pin hole where you want to anchor the chains. Mix and apply glue into one pin hole and let it stand for a few minutes.

33 Insert one eyepin stem into the hole and hold for few minutes until the glue sets. Repeat with the remaining eyepin.

Debbi Simon's jewelry designs have been featured in national magazines and books. Debbi is the author of *Crystal Chic*. She currently teaches mixed media and jewelry workshops in resin, epoxy clays, encaustic, and crystals nationally. Debbi studied art and design at the Milwaukee Institute of Art & Design (MIAD). After spending a few years in the design field, she decided that her passion was fine art and began painting seriously. She continually experiments with different media. An introduction to beads added jewelry designs to her mix.

debbisimon.com
create-your-style.com/Content.Node/
ambassadors/Debbi_Simon.en.php

"Learn your craft, and learn to finish and polish your designs well."

How long have you been making jewelry?

I have been an artist all my life, painting, selling, and teaching. I was fortunate to work for Kalmbach Publishing Co. and it was only natural for me to start designing jewelry as well. After having a few designs published, I started teaching, and the rest is history.

Best advice you've received?

I gravitate toward artists I admire and will take classes or ask advice from them. Over the years, I have gotten so much great feedback that is all relevant and important. I like to learn from the best and feel everyone has something to offer.

Favorite tool?

Two-part silicone mold material is my favorite. Since I work primarily in resin, epoxy clays, and wax, I love to make molds of everything, and I mean everything. Even in my paintings,

I have always been fascinated with textures, patterns, and ornamentation. Molds allow me to capture little relics along the way that I can add into my jewelry work.

Best thing about being an Ambassador?

I think most of all I love that Swarovski has valued and entrusted me to use, teach, and present their new products in my individual way as a designer. I have access to the best of the best and am told to play and create. As a designer, who could ask for more? The bonus has been working together with an extraordinary group of designers. We all have our strengths and draw energy from one another. It is great to be part of a group with such talent.

Favorite of the SWAROVSKI ELEMENTS?

My first loves were the opal colors. They attracted me to the possibilities

of working with crystals as a broad painting palette. My strength has always been my use of color. With every launch, I get to see great new products and, as always, the ideas start flowing. Based on the type of work I am doing now, the wide range of fancy stone shapes is appealing.

Inspiration?

Color, textures, and patterns; aged ornamentation and architecture; and other great artists.

Advice for new beaders?

Design what you love first … and you will find your style that will set you apart from the others. Learn your craft, and learn to finish and polish your designs well. Things like well-made loops, rivets, and crimps matter and will impact whether you are perceived as a professional designer or not. The mechanics will make your pieces look professional, and they are also the things others will be looking at.

Trashionista

Margot Potter

122

This idea has been bubbling around in my brain for a few years. I've done similar things with clear acrylic, but crystal takes it to a totally different level. It's a great way to upcycle those piles of magazines into something fabulous. The faceting on the crystals works beautifully to create a mosaic effect on the images. This could be taken in many directions. I added long and dramatic chain swags to this design, so it's not for everyday wear. You could opt for smaller swags or no chains at all for a more practical design. Personally, I love the drama and the sensuous movement of the chains across my hand.

materials

SWAROVSKI ELEMENTS

- 27mm 6656 galactic vertical pendant, Crystal
- 17mm 6240 wild heart pendant, Crystal Red Magma
- 3221 twist sew-on stones
    5 28mm Crystal Moonlight
    28mm Foiled Crystal

Other Supplies

- decoupage medium, matte finish
- 22-gauge German style jewelry wire, silver plated
- **5** 10mm oval thick connectors, silver tone
- **2** 10mm round connectors, silver tone
- **8** 10mm jump rings, silver tone
- swivel lobster clasp
- small chain, silver tone
- small rolo chain, silver tone
- magazines, for images

Tools

- roundnose pliers
- **2** pairs chainnose pliers
- bentnose pliers (optional)
- wire cutters
- scissors
- utility knife
- foam brush

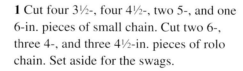

1 Cut four 3½-, four 4½-, two 5-, and one 6-in. pieces of small chain. Cut two 6-, three 4-, and three 4½-in. pieces of rolo chain. Set aside for the swags.

2 Select images small enough to be framed with crystal shapes. I used faces and eyes. Cut out images and adhere to the backs of the Crystal Moonlight twist stones with decoupage medium using a foam brush **(a)**. Paint a small coat of medium on the back of the image and allow to completely dry. Repeat with a second coat, again allowing to completely dry overnight. Don't blob medium on the front of the crystal. If you do, wipe with a wet cloth to remove.

3 Once the five beads are dry, use scissors to carefully cut the edges off of the images **(b)**. If there is any lifting of edges, add another coat of decoupage medium under and over the edge and allow to dry.

tip Paint the backs with a metallic paint or leafing pen for a dressier finish.

4 Use a utility knife to carefully remove any paper in the bead holes. If the paper lifts during this process, add a final layer of decoupage medium and allow to dry.

5 Use large oval connectors to connect beads **(c)**, including the Foiled Crystal twist stone. Work carefully so you don't break the crystals.

tip I added one foil-back crystal for design interest; you can use all images if you prefer.

6 Once the crystals are connected, check to be sure the connectors are secured. Add a round connector on each end bead.

7 Attach a jump ring and the clasp to the end connector on one end of the bracelet.

e

f

8 To attach the swags, start on one end. With a 10mm jump ring, connect a 5-, 4-, and a 3½-in. piece of small chain and the galactic pendant.

9 Swag the longest chain segment over to the connector between the second and third bead, and attach at this point with a

10mm jump ring (**d**). Before closing the jump ring, pick up a 3½-, a 4½-, and the 6-in. piece of chain.

10 Swag the longest chain over to the connector between the fourth and fifth beads, and attach at this point with a 10mm jump ring. Before closing the jump

ring, pick up a 3½-, 4½-, and 5-in. piece of chain.

11 Swag the 5-in. piece over to the connector at the end of the bracelet. Attach at this point with a 10mm jump ring. Before closing the jump ring, pick up a 4½- and a 3½-in. piece of chain.

note The center small chain swag is longer than the rest by design.

12 The second layer uses the rolo chain. Attach a 4-, 4½- and 6-in. piece of rolo chain to the 10mm jump ring on the connector between the first and second beads. Swag the longest piece over to the jump ring at the connector between the third and fourth beads.

13 Repeat step 12 between the third and fourth beads and swag the longest piece over to the connector between the fifth and sixth beads. Add a 4- and 4½- in. piece of rolo before closing the jump ring.

14 Check back through all jump rings to ensure they are closed with tension: Move the ends past one another as you are securing them closed and compress them until you hear and feel the click that tells you the ring is closed with tension.

15 To attach a wild heart dangle, make a small loop on the end of a 1½-in. piece of 22-gauge wire. Bend the loop 90 degrees. Thread this into the bead. Grasp the wire with a pair of roundnose pliers (**e**), and bend to form a coiled loop. Bend the coiled wire flush to the back of the bead to create a pendant. Open and close the link on the longer segment of the first rolo chain swag from the left side of the bracelet to attach the pendant (**f**).

tip It's really easy to make a coordinating pair of earrings and pendant necklace using the same techniques. Just connect a series of three crystals for the necklace with five varied lengths of chain, a galactic pendant, and a heart. For the earrings, face the eye images in opposite directions. Dangle three chain lengths and a single heart pendant beneath.

MARGOT

Margot Potter is an author, designer, writer, and TV personality. She has written seven jewelry-making books and has designed and consulted for some of the biggest names in the jewelry-making and craft industries. Margot creates vintage-inspired blogs for iLoveToCreate. She approaches everything with her signature sense of humor, boundless curiosity, and copious amounts of joie de vivre because she feels that if it's not fun, it's simply not worth doing. She invites people to not only think outside of the box, but to tear it up, repurpose it into something fabulous, and stand on it to reach for the stars. Equally comfortable at the writer's desk, in the design studio, on stage, or in front of the camera, Margot has creativity, moxie, and chutzpah to spare.

margotpotter.com.
create-your-style.com/Content.Node/
ambassadors/Margot-Potteren.php

"My best ideas always come from the times I'm willing to try something outrageous."

How long have you been making jewelry?
As a young teen I made jewelry; back then it was all about liquid silver and faux turquoise and coral necklaces! My real jewelry-making experience spans about 20 years. My husband and I had a retail store and I made exposed woven wire designs to sell. A wire manufacturer began buying them, and, even after we closed the store, the manufacturer kept asking for more. I realized that showing other people how to make jewelry might be the key to a new career, so I came up with a book concept, submitted a query to a publisher, and sold a book in two weeks. From there, my career took off.

Best advice you've received?
Learning how to crimp properly and use beading wire instead of fishing line was a big step for me when I was first starting out. Good technique is everything.

Favorite tool?
I can't pick a favorite tool! How could any jewelry designer pick just one? I use so many tools for so many purposes, and they all have a place in my heart. I do, however, feel my boundless creativity and my curious mind are my most important tools.

Best thing about being an Ambassador?
Working with crystal is a true passion of mine—one I've been sharing with my readers and fans from the start. It's an honor to be associated with the world's finest crystal and to have the insider's view of what's new and what's coming for the DIY market.

Favorite of the SWAROVSKI ELEMENTS?
I love them all because every element and every color, shape, and variation inspire new directions for my creativity. I like the big, bold pendants and I use the less obvious trimmings and sew-on stones in unexpected ways.

Inspiration?
I am endlessly interested in the world around me. Vintage magazines, gardens, nature, a walk through the hardware store, stories, poems, music, emotions—everything inspires me.

Advice for new beaders?
Master strong technique, get very good at constructing quality jewelry, and learn the basic rules of design. Once you have this foundation, let go of the need for perfection and welcome in the joy of creativity. My best ideas ALWAYS come from the times I'm willing to try something outrageous and stretch the materials in impossible directions. Within what others might call a mistake is the juicy stuff. You learn new things, you find out what works and what doesn't, and you discover your own style and direction. Be original. A good designer is inspired by others, but makes it her or his own.

Fluttering By

June Beach

I love butterflies. I love their grace, simplicity, and beauty. My love for all things vintage is certainly no secret, and it is something that is dear to my heart, so I created Fluttering By to showcase my love for both. Each has a separate voice, but they are simply beautiful together when combined into this necklace.

materials

SWAROVSKI ELEMENTS
- **2** 2058 flatback crystals, Sunflower
- **2** 12.5mm 5139 ring beads, Crystal Silver Night
- **5** 8mm 6128 crystal mini pears, Crystal Copper
- **14** 9X8mm 5826 crystal curved pearls, Powder Almond
- 12mm 5752 crystal clover bead, Sunflower
- 2854 butterfly flatbacks
    - 18mm Crystal Silver Night
    - 12mm Crystal
    - 8mm Crystal Red Magma
- 5810 Crystal Pearl
    - **7** 8mm Crystal Gold
    - **10** 4mm Crystal Bronze
- 5301 Xilion bicones
    - **5** 8mm Crystal AB
    - **4** 8mm Sunflower
    - **4** 6mm Crystal Bronze
    - **2** 4mm Sunflower
    - **5** 4mm Crystal Copper

Other supplies
- antique brass bookplate
- antique brass toggle
- antique brass chain
- **43** antique brass headpins
- **5** antique brass jump rings
- 22-gauge antique brass wire
- ICE resin
- mixing cups and stirrer
- Perfect Pearls pigment powder
- jewelry cement
- clear packing tape

Tools
- roundnose pliers
- chainnose pliers
- wire cutters

1 Place a piece of clear packing tape on the back of the bookplate. Make sure that the edges are sealed around the opening of the bookplate on the back.

2 Mix two-part resin per the manufacturers instructions.

3 Pour the resin into the opening of the bookplate. Lightly dust some of the Perfect Pearls powder into the resin. Use a toothpick to create a swirled effect.

4 Set the resin, but before it is fully cured, place the butterfly flatback crystal into the resin.

5 Let the resin cure completely per the manufacturer's instructions before removing the tape from the bookplate. Embellish the bookplate with flatback crystals (**a**).

6 Cut eight 8–12-link pieces of chain for the tassel.

7 Cut a 3-in. piece of wire and make a wrapped loop through the bottom section of the bookplate.

8 String the Sunflower clover bead onto the wire and make the first half of a larger wrapped loop below the bead.

9 Link the chain from step 6 to the loop and complete the wraps (**b**).

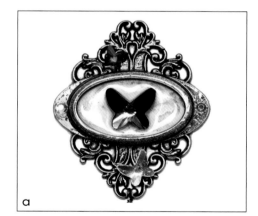
a

b

127

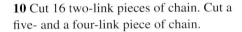

10 Cut 16 two-link pieces of chain. Cut a five- and a four-link piece of chain.

11 Trim the end from a headpin and make the first half of a wrapped loop. Connect the top of the bookplate and complete the wraps. String a curved pearl and make the first half of a wrapped loop. Connect a two-link chain piece and complete the wraps. Repeat on the other side of the bookplate **(c)**.

12 String a ring bead on a headpin, from the inside out. Make a plain loop and connect the end link of a chain from step 11. String another headpin through the remaining hole in the ring bead. Make a plain loop and connect a two-link piece of chain. Repeat on the other side of the necklace.

13 Continue to build each side of the necklace by connecting components and chain segments with wrapped-loop links. Attach in this order: Crystal Gold pearl, 4mm Sunflower crystal, curved pearl, 8mm Crystal AB, 8mm Crystal Gold pearl, and 4mm Sunflower crystal with a two-link section between each.

14 Connect a curved pearl to an end link of chain and to a five-link piece with a wrapped loop link. Repeat on the other end of the necklace with a four-link piece of chain.

15 Make a wrapped-loop link to attach a 4mm Crystal Bronze pearl to the end of one chain piece and half the toggle clasp. Repeat on the other end with the other clasp half **(d)**.

16 String the remaining crystals and pearls onto headpins and attach to the tassel with plain loops.

17 Use jump rings to attach the mini pear crystals to the tassel.

Your Fluttering By necklace is complete! Enjoy!

June Beach is the owner of Beach Haus Designs and The June Beach Collection. June has been designing jewelry and apparel for boutiques, department stores, and galleries, in addition to teaching jewelry design and merchandising classes, for over 20 years. June is one of the original CREATE YOUR STYLE with SWAROVSKI ELEMENTS Ambassadors and teaches jewelry design classes internationally in addition to conducting showroom product demonstrations and workshops. She has appeared on the television show *Beads, Baubles and Jewels* and has been published in magazines including *Seventeen, People Style Watch, Woman's World, Canadian Beading, Art Jewelry, Somerset Studio, Bead Design Studio,* and *Belle Armoire Jewelry.* June has worked as a successful designer, visual merchandiser, buyer, and product designer for apparel, jewelry, and accessories with some of the country's top retailers.

create-your-style.com/Content.Node/
ambassadors/June-Beach.en.php.

"Relax and enjoy the journey into the world of sparkles!"

How long have you been making jewelry?
I have been creating all my life but began making jewelry seriously about 10 years ago when I sold a bracelet on a whim to a customer. I realized then that I had something that not only I loved to do but others loved as well. It was a natural evolution for me.

Best advice you've received?
Never stop learning! I am surrounded by some amazing colleagues in this business and I am continually learning tips, tricks, and ideas from them.

Favorite tool?
I love my pliers and crochet hooks since I love, love, love, creating with wire: wirewrapping, crochet, Viking knit, and anything that has wire in it.

Best thing about being an Ambassador?
I am honored to be an ambassador and to be a part of a talented group that I respect and admire. What I like the most is that we are very close and are also incredibly supportive of each other. It is unique to be part of such a large group yet for it to feel so supportive, close-knit, and to find that everyone is protective of each other. The Ambassadors are the first to cheer successes—both personal and professional—as well as to be there when someone needs a shoulder to lean on. We have become friends and the group feels like family. Some of my best friends have come out of this honor and association. Thank you, Swarovski Elements!

Favorite of the SWAROVSKI ELEMENTS?
Honestly, I love them all! My favorite is the Antique Pink De-Art Pendants and the Astral Pink Designer Edition Hearts. I love the cut of the crystal and I think the colors are simply beautiful!

Inspiration?
I am inspired by traveling; I am constantly taking pictures. A row of old bikes, butterflies, the desert cactus in bloom, an ancient tea house in Asia, the great ocean road, bathing boxes, the Eiffel tower, window shopping in New York—I love seeing how that sunset on Lake Michigan I witnessed can turn into a color story that becomes a statement necklace that mirrors that special moment.

Advice for new beaders?
Take classes! Learn how to do the basics correctly and then create, design, and explore the fabulous world of jewelry. To feel confident in what you are doing and to put your own signature style or touch onto a design is an amazing feeling. Relax and enjoy the journey into the world of sparkles!

Simply Toggles

Diane Hertzler

This elegant and modular bracelet uses the same techniques for each component. This perfectly symmetrical bracelet is simply a series of toggles: Circular peyote stitch is used to create the three-dimensional forms connected to the Chessboard Buttons, and the buttons are embellished with Xilion beads.

materials

SWAROVSKI ELEMENTS
- **7** 21x11mm 3093 chessboard rectangle crystal buttons, Crystal
- **42** 3mm 5328 crystal bicones, Purple Velvet

Other supplies
- **7** grams 11º cylinder beads, A (teal DB 1764)
- **4** grams 11º cylinder beads, B (purple DB 609)
- **2** grams 11º cylinder beads, C (silver DB 41)
- **30** 2mm or 11º seed beads, D (silver)
- **.5** gram 15º seed beads, E (teal, 17A)
- #10 beading needles
- Nylon beading thread, size B; or Fireline, 4 lb. test

Tools
- magnetic board and ruler to hold graph

Overview

Using circular peyote stitch with two different increase techniques, create a four-sided, three-dimensional form. Add strength with a second layer of beads. Sew a button to the end and embellish with crystals and seed beads. Repeat to create six more forms. Slide each button through the hole of the next form to create a chain.

Let's Get Started

note Each form is shaped like a kite. The increase at the bottom will be referred to as a herringbone stitch to make a corner. A firm tension is necessary to create a stiff form.

First Layer

1 Thread a needle with a comfortable length of thread. Pick up 39 11ºs in this order: B, A, B, C, B, A, B, A, B, A, B, A, B, A, B, A, C, C, A, B, A, B, A, B, A, B, A, B, A, B, C, B, A, B, A, B, C, B, A. Slide the beads down the thread leaving a 6-in. tail. These beads will sit to form

the first two rounds as the third round is added. Sew through the first bead strung to begin round 3 (**figure 1, a–b**).

2 Work rounds 3–7 as follows:
Round 3
- Work one peyote stitch with an A.
- Work an increase: Pick up two Cs, skip the C in the previous round, and sew through the following bead (**b–c**).
- Work six peyote stitches with As (**c–d**).
- Work a herringbone stitch with two Cs to make the corner (**d–e**).
- Work six peyote stitches with As (**e–f**).
- Work an increase with two Cs, and then work two peyote stitches with As.
- Work an increase with two Cs, work one

peyote stitch with an A, and then step up to begin the next round (**f–g**).

Round 4
- Work one peyote stitch with an A. Pick up a C, and sew through the next C in the previous round (**g–h**).
- Work seven peyote stitches with As, and then work a herringbone stitch with two Cs at the corner.
- Work seven peyote stitches with As, pick up a C, and sew through the next C.
- Work three peyote stitches with As, pick up a C, and sew through the next C.
- Work two peyote stitches with As, and step up (**h–i**).

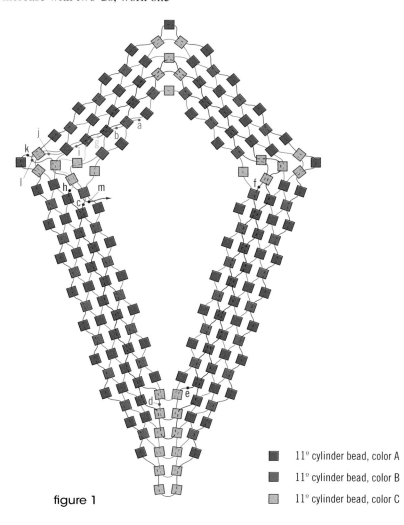

figure 1

■ 11º cylinder bead, color A

■ 11º cylinder bead, color B

▨ 11º cylinder bead, color C

- ■ 11º cylinder bead, color A
- ■ 11º cylinder bead, color B
- □ 11º cylinder bead, color C
- ○ 2 mm bead, color D
- • 15º seed bead, color E
- ◆ 3 mm bicone crystal
- ▱ 21 mm x 11 mm crystal button

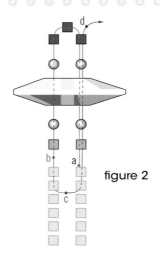

figure 2

figure 3

Round 5
- Work nine peyote stitches with As, and then work a herringbone stitch with two Cs at the corner.
- Work 15 peyote stitches with As, and step up (i–j).

Round 6
- Work an increase with two Cs, and then work eight peyote stitches with Bs.
- Work a herringbone stitch with two Cs at the corner, and then work eight peyote stitches with Bs.
- Work an increase with two Cs, and then work three peyote stitches with Bs. Repeat these four stitches to complete the row, and step up (j–k).

Round 7
- Pick up an A, and sew through the next C.
- Work nine peyote stitches with As, and then work a herringbone stitch with two Cs at the corner.
- Work nine peyote stitches with As.
- Pick up an A, sew through the next C, and then work four peyote stitches with As. Repeat these five stitches once (k–l), but do not step up.
- Sew through the Cs to exit the first B added in round 2 (l–m).

note Rounds 8–10 will sit on top of rows 3–5. Round 8 will be sewn to round 2, round 9 will be sewn to round 8, and round 10 will be sewn to round 9 and zipped to round 6.

3 Work a second layer as follows:

Round 8
- Pick up an A, and sew through the next bead in round 2. Repeat this stitch five times.
- Work a herringbone stitch with two Cs at the corner.
- Pick up an A, and sew through the next B. Repeat this stitch five times.
- Pick up two Cs; sew through the next B.
- Pick up an A, and sew through the next B. Repeat this stitch.
- Pick up two Cs, and sew through the next B. Pick up an A and sew through the next B. Repeat this stitch. Pick up two Cs, sew through the next B, and step up through the first A added in this round.

Round 9
- Work six peyote stitches with As, and then work a herringbone stitch with two Cs at the corner.
- Work seven peyote stitches with As, pick up a C, and sew through the next C in the previous round.
- Work three peyote stitches with As, pick up a C, and sew through the next C in the previous round.
- Work three peyote stitches with As.
- Pick up a C and sew through the next C.
- Work one peyote stitch with an A and step up through the first A added in this round.

Round 10
- Work a round of tubular peyote with an A in each stitch except the corner, where you will work a herringbone stitch with two Cs. Step up.
- Zip up round 10 to round 6, and end the threads.

Attach the Button
Sew through the beadwork to exit the first C added in the herringbone stitch in round 7.

4 Pick up a C and a D. Sew through the hole in the button from back to front. Pick up a D, three As, and a D. Sew through the second hole in the button from front to back. Pick up a D and a C (figure 2, a–b).

5 Sew down through two Cs in the corner (b–c).

6 Sew back up through two Cs in the corner, the first C and D added in this step, the button, the second D, and the first A (c–d).

Button Fringe Embellishment
note Add two crystal fringes to each A on top of the button for a total of six crystals.

7 Pick up a 3mm bicone and an E. Skip the E, and sew back through the crystal (figure 3, a–b).

8 Sew through the A again in the same direction (b–c).

9 Repeat steps 1 and 2 to add a second crystal to the A (c–d).

10 Sew through the next A, and create two more fringes as in steps 1–3.

11 Repeat step 4 for the remaining A.

12 Sew through the D, the button from front to back, and the D and two Cs directly below. End the thread.

DIANE

Diane Hertzler began beading about 20 years ago after trying her hand at every other type of art or craft that used a needle. Over the years, she began creating her own designs, which have been published in many outlets. She is best known for her jewelry and ornament designs using SWAROVSKI ELEMENTS and Delica beads. In 2009, Diane's joint bracelet project with Wendy Hitchins, of Australia, for Convergence: Jewelry Designs Inspired by the Four Elements, was accepted into the traveling exhibit, and was published in Convergence by the International Society of Glass Beadmakers, and Jewelry Designs with Art Glass Beads, by *Bead&Button*. Diane and craft-loving husband, Bob, live with their dog Apache in Mount Gretna, Penn.

dianehertzler.com
create-your-style.com/Content.Node/
ambassadors/Diane-Hertzler.en.php

"Beading will be more enjoyable if you attempt projects within your skill range and advance at a comfortable pace."

How long have you been making jewelry?
I have been beading and designing jewelry since the early 1990s. I would consider bead design and teaching more of a passion than a livelihood.

Best advice you've received?
When investing a great deal of time and effort in a project, use the very best materials possible. That is why I was attracted to SWAROVSKI ELEMENTS and precious metal findings.

Favorite tool?
Needle and thread—with all of the crafts and hobbies that I have tried, I always return to needle and thread projects, especially beading.

Best thing about being an Ambassador?
The Ambassadors are supportive, friendly, and very helpful to me in my pursuits, and I am thrilled to be part of this program.

Favorite of the SWAROVSKI ELEMENTS?
I like beads, buttons, and sew-on elements because they work well with my design style.

Inspiration?
Sometimes the colors and forms that I see in nature when I travel, sometimes lyrics or titles of songs, and sometimes the elements and colors themselves will trigger my creativity.

Advice for new beaders?
New beaders will achieve more success and therefore enjoyment if they become involved with the how-to literature and classes that are available. Beading will also be more enjoyable if you attempt projects within your skill range, and then advance at a comfortable pace.

Glamour of Night
Naomi Yogo
Japan
create-your-style.com/Content.Node/
ambassadors/Naomi-Yogo.php

Pink and Blue Flourish Necklace
Oluseyi Abdullahi
Nigeria
create-your-style.com/Content.Node/
ambassadors/Oluseyi-Abdullahi.php

Mad Hatter
(iPad case)
Kellie DeFries
United States
create-your-style.com/
Content.Node/
ambassadors/
Kellie-DeFries.php

Provence Garden
Susan Ho
Taiwan
create-your-style.com/
Content.Node/
ambassadors/
Susan-Ho.en.php

Heather Laithwaite
South Africa
create-your-style.com/Content.Node/
ambassadors/Heather-Laithwaite.en.php

The Circle of the Triangle
Talia Rutenberg
Israel
create-your-style.com/Content.Node/
ambassadors/Talia-Rutenberg.php

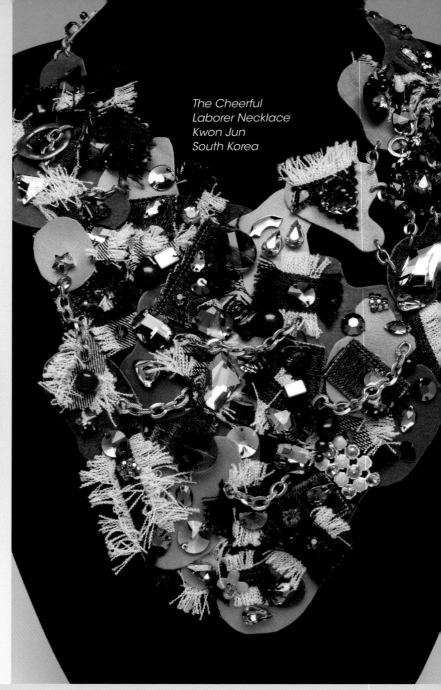

The Cheerful
Laborer Necklace
Kwon Jun
South Korea

Tyra
Fabienne Vandervaeren
Belgium
create-your-style.com/
Content.Node/ambassadors/
Fabienne-Van-Isterdael-
Vandervaeren.en.php

Swing Carousel
Yuka Kaede
Japan
create-your-style.com/Content.Node/
ambassadors/Yuka-Kaede.php

139

Knotting Bracelet
I-Chuan Lee
Taiwan
create-your-style.com/Content.Node/ambassadors/I-Chuan-Lee.en.php

Little Amazonia
Un-Roen Manarata
Belgium
create-your-style.com/Content.Node/
ambassadors/Un-Roen-Manarata.en.php

Ophelia
Necklace
Lee Jong Rye
Korea
create-your-style.com/Content.Node/
ambassadors/Rachel-Jong–Rye–Lee.php

Iznik
Petra Tismer
Germany
create-your-style.com/Content.Node/
ambassadors/Petra-Tismer.php

Madras
Jean Campbell
United States
create-your-style.com/
Content.Node/
ambassadors/
Jean-Campbell.en.php

French Cancan
Alicante Chassagne
France
create-your-style.com/
Content.Node/ambassadors/
Alicante-Chassagne.php

Maiko Ball Pendant
Saori Abe-Schroeder
Germany
create-your-style.com/
Content.Node/ambassadors/
Saori-Abe-Schroeder.php

Big Beauty
Sabine Lippert
Germany
create-your-style.com/
Content.Node/ambassadors
Sabine-Lippert.php

Shower of Blossoms
Sonoko Nozue
Japan
create-your-style.com/Content.Node/
ambassadors/Sonoko-Nozue.php